Up Your Productivity

Up Your Productivity

Kurt Hanks

Crisp Publications, Inc.
Los Altos, California

Other books by the author

Wake Up Your Creative Genius
Kurt Hanks and Jay Parry

Rapid Viz   A New Method for the Rapid Visualization of Ideas
Kurt Hanks and Larry Belliston

Draw!   A Visual Approach to Learning, Thinking and Communicating
Kurt Hanks and Larry Belliston

Design Yourself!
Kurt Hanks, Larry Belliston, and Dave Edwards

Printed in the United States of America

Library of Congress Cataloging-in-Publication Data

Hanks, Kurt, 1947-
  Up your productivity.

  Includes index.
  1. Labor productivity.   2. Management.   I. Title.
HD57.H325   1986   658.3'14   86-7294
ISBN 0-931961-49-1

Contents

Warning

This is not a typical kind of business book. I think many business books are too big, too hard to read, and sometimes even boring. I decided to create a business book that's different, one made for easy reading, one that would be entertaining and fun to read even though its purpose is serious.

You don't even have to read it in the order in which the pages happen to be numbered. Most readers will, I believe, be able to recognize and choose the tips and insights that best serve their interests. For example, look back at the Contents to choose the topic you are most interested in, and turn to that topic first.

Although this book is meant to be fun, it is built on proven ideas and methods, and it reflects my own experiences. It will, I hope, help you make your business more productive.

KURT HANKS

Kurt Hanks

This Book Can Help Your Productivity

This book can help the manager see solutions where before there was only uncertainty or blackness and despair.

I won't lie to you. People hassles never end. As long as you are a manager, you'll have to deal with people problems. And you'll have to deal with time management and hiring the right employees. And with corporate competitors and new trends in the marketplace. That's the bad news.

But there is some good news: It's possible to deal with a lot of these problems in a constructive, conclusive way. By using the ideas in this book, you can increase your sanity level and decrease your hassles.

And here's even better news: You don't have to use *all* the ideas in this book to win some real benefits. Pick the ones that will help you most now. You'll find that they work—and they can work immediately to increase the productivity of you and your employees.

Do you need help increasing productivity? Turn the page, and you'll find all kinds of useful ideas!

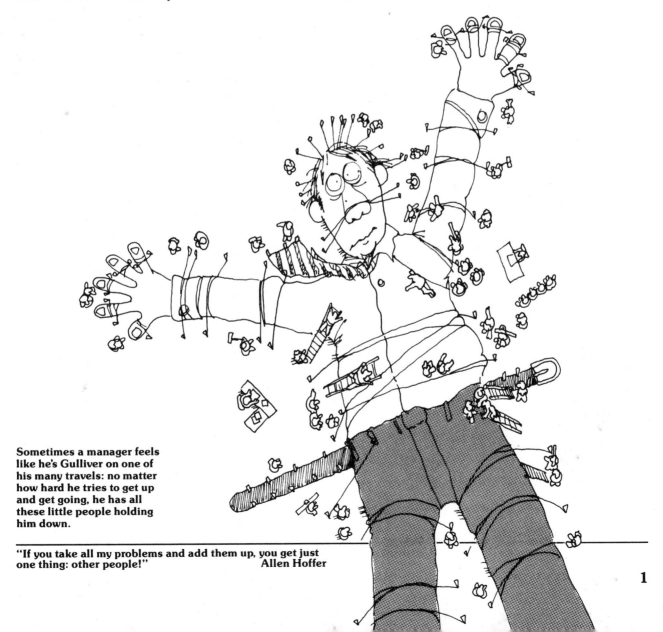

Sometimes a manager feels like he's Gulliver on one of his many travels: no matter how hard he tries to get up and get going, he has all these little people holding him down.

"If you take all my problems and add them up, you get just one thing: other people!"
Allen Hoffer

1

The People Hassle

The people hassle drastically decreases productivity.

A Never-ending Challenge

A manager's job is a daily succession of never-ending problems. Pressures close in from all sides. You're up to your nose in a river of problems—and you're about to go under!

What They Say

Whatever company a manager's in, his problems are the same. They fit together into one great big continual hassle. Here's what managers are saying:

"Workers never follow instructions. We go over it again and again, and just when I think they've finally got it, they go and do it another way."

"I got as much water as I could."

"Here's just what you asked for—the shortest memo possible."

"The monthly production level is down. My boss is on my back to raise it. Top management is on my back because the approved methods aren't working. My workers are on my back because they're doing the best they can. And all I end up with is an aching back!"

"What, another irate customer? Just what are they doing down there in customer relations—giving them obscene hand signals?"

"Ah hah! I caught you!"

"Those bureaucrats only look down long hollow tubes. Why can't they look at reality instead of at their stupid rules?"

"I call a meeting and openly ask for honest feedback. All the workers say everything's fine—then they go out and continue stabbing each other in the back."

"You do great work!"

"You did an outstanding job!"

"I love board meetings! Everyone gives his two cents worth and then expects me to treat it like it's worth a million bucks."

"They have a bunch of radios out there in the shop, and each one is playing a different tune. And the whole group of them dresses like rejects from a Hell's Angels gang."

"Why do I have to keep saying the same thing over and over? It's in the policy manual. Can't they read?"

Higher levels of productivity are directly linked to people. By decreasing your people problems and increasing your use of these people, you'll invariably get better productivity.

A manager's problems are mainly people problems. In the end, if you can solve your problems with people, you'll be solving the biggest of all your problems.

The Manager Hassle

- Joan was a stutterer. It was a real problem for her, and she hated the embarrassment of being unable to express what she wanted to. When she got excited, she stuttered more and more until finally she choked up and couldn't talk at all. And the more she tried to control the problem, the worse it got.

- The human body has an autonomic system that runs breathing, heartbeat, and other vital functions. The autonomic functions are all unconscious—nobody can control them with his conscious brain (including, despite popular tradition, the yogis and swamis of India). If a person were given conscious control over his autonomic system, he'd die. It would be too much for him to keep track of.

- It was Henry's first time on a horse, and he was nervous. He grasped the reins firmly with his hands and pulled. "Giddyup," he said. The horse made a move to go forward, and Henry pulled back on the reins even more. His palms were sweating. "Giddyup," he said again. The bit pulled into the horse's mouth, and the horse could do nothing other than stand there and shake.

How are these three situations like the following manager's?

Jerry was the manager of a wholesale auto parts warehouse. He was afraid of losing control over his people, so he raised the level of control he exercised. He required a filled-out time log every day, written reports once a week, interviews once a month. But the more he tightened the screws on his people, the more they rebelled. And the more they rebelled, the more concerned he became, so he tightened the screws even more. It was a vicious cycle.

Productivity began to drop. Eventually it might have frozen up, and the warehouse might have had to close down.

Some managers try to entice their people—and drive them at the same time.

When control gets too tight in any situation, things will oscillate until finally they totally freeze up. When that happens, control is lost completely, and the controller is left with nothing to control.

If you set the tolerances on a thermostat too tightly, the heat will go on, off, on, off, and on in a very short sequence. The thermostat will chatter back and forth until it wears out, at which point it will freeze up. And then you'll have no control whatever over the heat in the room.

People are the same as thermostats. Try to control them too tightly, and you'll eventually lose control altogether.

The Little Red Wagon

Jeff bought a little red wagon for his seven kids and turned them loose to play with it. They laughed and shouted as they climbed in for a ride. Jeff watched from the window. Three kids on the wagon, five, seven. Seven little kids all squashed into a two-kid wagon, all waiting for a ride, with no one to pull them.

The laughter soon turned to tears. They began to argue. The older kids told the younger ones to get off and pull. "Come on! We can't have any fun."

People need room to move around in.

At first the kids all piled in, with no one to pull. But they worked the problem out for themselves.

"We're too little," the younger kids responded at the tops of their voices.

Jeff was tempted to go out and supervise. Maybe the kids were too little to work out the problem. Maybe he should have bought them *two* wagons. But instead of controlling things from his adult perspective, he decided to watch for a while longer to see what the kids would do.

Before long the oldest kids were out of the wagon and were pulling the others down the street. The next trip, some of the older ones got to ride. They had divided the tasks equally among the seven, taking into consideration the age, size, and strength of each child. They spent the next several hours riding and pulling each other, and everyone got a fair chance to ride. Everyone had a great time.

But what do you suppose would have happened if daddy had gone out there with rules and control?

"Get Out of the Way!"

Bell Laboratories is one of the most successful research institutes in the world. Workers at the labs have won numerous Nobel Prizes for their technological innovation. The labs are constantly being studied as models of creative and productive excellence. The secret to their success? They refuse to exert too much control over their people. Said Arno Penzias, research vice-president at Bell Labs:

"The way to run this place is to hire smart people and then get out of their way."

How to Do It

It doesn't work to totally relinquish all control. The best approach is to be tight in the ends you hope to achieve but loose in the means that are used to reach these ends. The manager should take careful control of setting goals, for instance, and should see that everything the company does points itself to these goals. But the specific approaches individual members use to reach the goals should be more open.

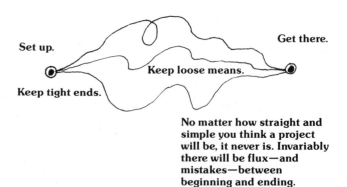

Set up.

Keep tight ends.

Keep loose means.

Get there.

No matter how straight and simple you think a project will be, it never is. Invariably there will be flux—and mistakes—between beginning and ending.

A good manager spends a lot of time setting things up and making sure everyone has a good picture of what's expected. Then he lets his people go to work.

Death by Institutionalization

You know your company has a problem when it takes a great number of people to do a simple task.

BACK UP #17

Symptoms of the Disease

When an organization becomes an end in itself, rather than a means to an end, paralysis and possibly death are near. This process of an institution becoming its own end is called *institutionalization.**

When a person catches a fatal disease, he often struggles with it as it slowly takes him to death. And, as death approaches, more and more of his resources (time, energy, money) are spent trying to maintain his life.

It's no different with an organization. And as death approaches, the organization will sap the strength of all around.

"Most hierarchies are nowadays so cumbered with rules and traditions, and so bound in by public laws, that even high employees do not have to lead anyone anywhere, in the sense of pointing out the direction and setting the pace. They simply follow precedents, obey regulations, and move at the head of the crowd. Such employees *lead* only in the sense that the carved wooden figurehead leads the ship."
Laurence J. Peter

Here are the ten danger signals to watch for:

1. A deepening fear of anything that questions.

2. A growing intolerance for anything out of line.

3. The term *old* becomes ever more applicable.

4. Individual initiative is an increasing pain in the neck.

5. A spreading belief that all wisdom, light, and knowledge come from on high.

6. A growing obsession with numbers.

7. A proliferation of rules and rule breakers.

8. More and more accomplishes less and less.

9. Communication is increasingly done by "ventriloquism," i.e., without personal interactions.

10. An increased standardization of the trivial.

* This is just a long word meaning that many people are doing what a few people could do better.

> ## "The purpose of an organization is to enable ordinary human beings to do extraordinary things."
>
> **Peter Drucker**

History of the Illness

An organization is most productive when it is a means to an end. It should be a tool to build and to accomplish something. It shouldn't be a tyrant, dominating all for its own self-centered ego. When it becomes that, not only is it not productive, but it becomes a destroyer. It becomes an end in itself.

Many organizations start out with a spark of hope, an idea, and little else! But the lack of funds and the pressures against it are slowly overcome by the power of the people and their growing obsession to see it survive. It becomes a dynamic, living enterprise, and you can see that life on the faces of those involved.

But somewhere along the journey between birth and the *Fortune* 500, the people's creation starts to turn on them. It turns into a Frankenstein monster that feeds on the altruism of those involved.

The company becomes a law unto itself having a perfect view of the universe and all that is in it. Anything else is of little value or the work of moronic heretics. It fails to see the little cracks; after all, they are so small. It fails to heed the voices of warning; after all, they are but whispers. As the cracks get bigger, the eyesight grows dimmer. As the voices grow louder, the ears grow weaker.

When the company loses the spirit of its beginnings, and its sole purpose is its own survival, the buzzards start circling above—because something very precious down below has died.

Vicious Spiral of Behavior

Caught in a Vicious Spiral

Kathleen was having hard times as a sales manager. Every day she'd go to work and give her salespeople a good pep talk: "Get out there and get them!" she'd say. "Check out those referrals. Increase your customer list."

But every day the salespeople would perform just as they had before. Sales were decreasing—and Kathleen was starting to worry about her job security.

Kathleen's problem was that she was caught in a vicious spiral. The spiral held her in its clutches so that she couldn't get out. She wanted to try another approach, but she didn't know how. All she knew was the way she'd done things in the past.

The vicious spiral is a common enemy of productivity:

- **Allen** is suffering job burnout. It's all he can do to go to work every morning. His boss doesn't make matters any better. Allen is stuck in the spiral, and his boss is keeping him there. "Allen, you

People who get caught in a vicious cycle of behavior find it difficult to get out. Instead, they just repeat the same behavior patterns over and over again.

The more a person walks over the same old territory, the deeper his rut grows.

"You've got to do better!"

"Your performance stinks!"

"I'm doing just fine!"

"You can't fire me. Don't forget my sister is on the board of directors!"

should do this now. Then do this. Then do that."

"I sure wish he'd take a little initiative," the boss says. But he can't—he's stuck in the spiral.

- **Mom** has a daily struggle with Becky in the two hours before school. "Make your bed," she says at eight o'clock.

At eight-ten she checks up on Becky: "Have you made your bed? Go make it!"

At eight-fifteen: "Haven't you got that bed made yet? I can't believe it!"

"Get up there and make your bed. NOW!"

At eight-eighteen: "I'm not going to tell you again. Get up there and make that bed!"

At eight-thirty: "I'm going to go up and check your bed now, and it sure better be made!"

At eight-thirty-one: "All right! You're in trouble, young lady!"

And so on. It's the vicious spiral, and neither Mom nor Becky is having much luck at getting out of it. And of course Mom ends up making the bed every day.

- **The management at Woodworks, Inc.,** is having the same problem. "We've got to have better customer relations," the boss says. "You've got to do a heck of a lot better, people."

COMPLAINTS

"You've got to have better customer relations!"

"Yeah, yeah," the people respond.

Then they go on doing what they were doing before. They're all stuck in the vicious spiral.

Can you imagine how devastating the spiral can be to productivity in all its forms?

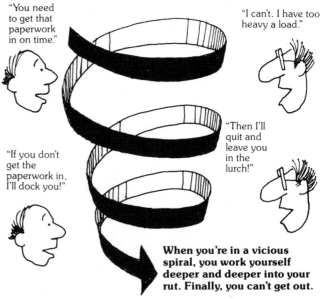

"You need to get that paperwork in on time."

"I can't. I have too heavy a load."

"If you don't get the paperwork in, I'll dock you!"

"Then I'll quit and leave you in the lurch!"

When you're in a vicious spiral, you work yourself deeper and deeper into your rut. Finally, you can't get out.

As long as we persist in our old, nonproductive ways of doing things, we'll be stuck in a vicious spiral and be unable to improve. And if everyone is sharing the same frame of reference, the problem will be even worse. It will persist and intensify. Attempted solutions to the problem won't make any difference.

You've probably seen the spiral in your work or home. The boss or the mom or dad says, "Let's try this new approach." Everyone agrees. But it doesn't make any difference. Two weeks later it's, "Let's try this approach now." And everyone gives it a good try. But nothing takes.

Only one solution will work: The people stuck in the spiral must change their frame of reference. Band-Aids won't work here—what's called for is major surgery. The old game needs to be replaced with a new one.

- **Randy** desperately needed to get in touch with a writing collaborator who was a

Getting stuck in a rut is more dangerous now than it's ever been. Things are changing so rapidly in the world that internal change is becoming increasingly critical.

professor. He called the professor at work. She wasn't there, but the secretary was happy to take a message. He called the professor's home. The professor wasn't there either, but her husband was happy to take a message. But the professor never returned the calls.

Every other day Randy called his professor friend, but he could never get in touch. He was stuck in a vicious spiral, and he knew it. Finally he decided to change the frame of reference. He had been calling and saying, "This is Randy. Please have the professor call." So he changed and said, "This is Captain Wilson. It's urgent that I speak with the professor."

As you might imagine, we all had a good laugh when Randy hung up!

That approach was a little deceptive. Randy was *not* a Captain Wilson. But it got results. The professor jumped to the conclusion that the police were calling her about something. Suddenly she wasn't too busy to return his calls. The professor called back within five minutes.

Getting Out of the Spiral

- **Allen's boss** wants him to take initiative. He changes his direction to break out of the spiral. "Here's a job you need to do," the boss says. "I don't care how you do it; that's entirely up to you."

- **Mom** is tired of fighting Becky about making her bed every morning. And she's tired of ending up making it herself. So she changes direction. She stuffs her mouth full of soda crackers and, breathing heavily, proceeds to make the bed smooth and neat. With crackers all over the sheets. After two days of sleeping in a crumby bed, Becky decides to make her own bed. Mom didn't have to say another word.

- **The managers at Woodworks, Inc.,** want better customer relations, but their workers just don't seem to get the message. So they change directions to get out of their vicious spiral. They have each of the workers visit several other businesses *as customers* to see how they like to be treated. Suddenly their customer relations improve.

"Thanks. You don't know how long I've worked for this."

"Congratulations on being appointed to the board."

If you get caught in a rut, there's only one thing to do: shift your actions into another direction.

If no results here, then . . .   concentrate efforts here.

The best way to break out of a vicious spiral is to change directions.

The only way out of a vicious spiral digging a deeper and deeper rut is a change in location.

The man and his boss both move out of the rut with changing conditions—now the man is on an equal footing with his sister!

Three Steps toward Needed Change

Once you've recognized the need for change in your organization, it's time to take action. But what do you do? This book will give you many ideas. Your own brain can give you many others. But you need to get these ideas out.

Three steps to getting the ideas you need:

Step 1

Get a pen and paper. Then go to a place where you won't be disturbed by anything or anybody.

You often need to get away from your job and from other people in order to be able to think clearly.

Step 2

Sit down and list all the things that slow your company down, that keep you from being more productive. Don't worry about the quality of your ideas; you want to go for quantity. Write as many ideas as you can, as fast as you can, until you've filled up one side of the page. Leave a little space between each entry; you'll use that space on the next step.

Step 3

Now, using the blank space you left on the page, write three things you can do to solve each of the problems you listed. After you've written your solutions, list each one in order of priority and then ACT.

ACTION is the most critical part. Without it, everything else is a waste of time.

After you've made your list, filter out the dross and form a clear statement of what each problem is. Be sure to go after the problem, not its symptoms.

You should be able to come up with lots of ideas. Most of them won't work, but you need only one to enjoy a breakthrough.

Success depends on getting away from it all, finding a place where you can be alone. This is a simple thing—so simple that we often fail to do it.

Biting Off More Than You Can Chew

Be careful what you bite into; it may bite back.

Too often we let foggy perceptions, based on false premises, obscure what we can and cannot do. We see things as we want them to be, not as they really are. The result is that we bite off more than we can chew—and when we do that, we usually end up gagging on it!

Foggy Perceptions

In 1982, Braniff Airlines shocked the business world by declaring bankruptcy. The cause? They bit off more than they could chew. After the federal government deregulated the airline industry in 1978, Braniff began to expand at an incredible rate. They moved into new areas, trying to get more routes and more customers. They went into a price war with other airlines.

In Braniff's effort to make the golden goose produce more eggs, they killed it off!

The problem of foggy perceptions and false premises plagues people in every area of their lives. It runs from their home lives to their business lives and even into their recreation. Usually their work and the rest of their worlds are going backward, rather than forward.

Invincible Jesse

Jesse James was on the top of the world. He was one of the most wanted criminals in the United States. He had acquired tens of thousands of dollars through his bank and stage robberies. He invented the art of train robbery. Apparently he began to think he was invincible, because in 1876 he bit off more than he could chew. He and seven other gang members attempted to rob the First National Bank at Northfield, Minnesota. Of the eight robbers, only two escaped—Jesse and his brother, Frank. The other six were either killed or captured.

So much for the famous James gang. They were done in by trying to bite off more than they could chew.

"Can-Do" People

Too many of our businesses today are run by macho men and wonder women. These are "can-do" people who figure that "nothing's impossible as long as you believe." That kind of attitude is fine for a Hollywood musical, but in the real world we need to deal with reality. There are limits for every business. There's a place where every gang should stop.

Whenever we start something new, we need to take a good look at every aspect of it. The crucial question to ask is this: "Is the direction I'm heading in leading me into a situation I won't be able to handle?"

A Murphy Cushion

Murphy's law reigns supreme throughout society. For example, here's how one of the greatest weapons of all time worked:

In World War II, the Russians got the great idea of the dog mine. They trained dogs to think there was delicious food underneath tanks. The idea was that the dogs would run under the advancing German tanks—complete with the bombs the Russians strapped to their backs. When the dog and the tank came in contact—Ka-boom!

But the trainers forgot Murphy's law. They entered their first battle, strapped the bombs on the dogs—and watched in horror as the dogs promptly ran *from* the German tanks straight toward the Russian tanks. The dogs had been trained well, but only with Russian tanks. An entire Russian division was forced into rapid retreat. That was the first and last day they used the dog mines.

Bomber Bats

A similar fate befell the bomber bats that the Americans tried. Someone got the bright idea that the military could strap tiny bombs to bats, then drop the bats over Japan. The bats would then fly down to earth and set up house under the eaves of Japanese houses—where the bombs would explode.

When they took a batch of bats up for their first test run, Murphy's law entered in. The bats were asleep when they were dropped, and some didn't wake up. They dropped straight to the earth "like tiny kamikazes," according to *Time* on April 5, 1982. Others simply flew off and were never heard from again.

But all was not lost. One found a place to stay nearby and blew it up. It was the supervising general's car!

This is the only photograph ever taken of Murphy. It's a self-portrait, taken with a camera that had a timer.

The Power of Murphy

Murphy, the founder of Murphy's law, has got to be one of the most powerful people who ever lived. He has his finger in every pie. It doesn't matter what you're working on, Murphy and his law just have to get involved.

Part of the reason is that Murphy's law is so universal. It applies to every imaginable situation. Murphy's law goes like this:

If anything can go wrong, it will.

Then there are corollaries:

Everything always takes longer than you expect.

Nothing is ever as simple as it seems.

If several things could possibly go wrong, the thing that will go wrong is the worst.

If everything seems to be going along well, you've obviously overlooked something.

A Murphy Cushion

There are times when organizations must grow and change in order to survive. They have to try new approaches, processes, ideas, concepts, people, and technology. But anything new is unknown, and anything unknown usually contains hidden problems. Hope for the best, and anticipate the worst when it comes to trying anything new, because Murphy's law is a law of life.

The only solution is this: **Anytime you're trying something new, construct a cushion to protect yourself.** Build yourself a Murphy cushion, which will separate you from the harmful results of Murphy's law. (This is not to be confused with a whoopie cushion.) Only with a Murphy cushion will you be able to make the necessary change and still live through it.

A cushion is a great device to prevent unforeseen problems.

Some kinds of Murphy cushions to use:

- **Allow enough time.** One government report was due by June 30, and it was critical that it be on time. The preparers thought they were allowing enough time, but they didn't figure on the review after review it had to go through. Murphy's law got them. The report was late, costing the government (and thus the taxpayers) millions of dollars in late interest fees.

- **Provide enough money.** If you're going to Europe on vacation, a ticket that will take you across the Atlantic isn't enough. You need one that will take you all the way there and all the way back. New endeavors eat up money at an alarming rate, and it's often hard to know in advance how much will be needed. The answer: Have a good cash cushion to take care of unforeseen expenses.

- **Plan for the unexpected.** If you haven't done something before, you probably don't know everything you should expect. Think of everything that could possibly go wrong, and plan for some others you didn't think of.

A man was once taking a journey through a dark and dangerous forest. He planned and prepared for everything: getting lost, wild animals, marauding bands of robbers, breaking his leg. But Murphy's law got him with the unexpected. One night he was knocked cold by a rock. His horse had slipped on the rough ground and flipped a rock into the air. The rock had bounced off a tree onto the traveler's head.

- **Proceed with caution.** Sit down slowly, or you may find yourself punctured by the tacks of Murphy's law. Because a competitor had just opened a new branch for printing books, a small printing firm rushed out to open their own new book branch. They didn't feel like they had time to do market research before they went out to fight the competition—and they found out the hard way that the market would not support a second book printer.

To use the cushion, grasp it firmly with both hands and let yourself be seated.

Warning: As you sit on the cushion, go down slowly!

- **Keep a healthy skepticism.** The world is full of new stuff just waiting to be tried—and much of it is useless or worse. Often a new solution proposed for your problems can cost more than the problem itself. So sometimes the best solution is to do nothing at all. By holding fast to your present position, you at least know something about how to avoid the worst effects of Murphy's law. Sometimes a healthy skepticism is the best cushion of all.

NOTE: Some situations are so cursed by Murphy that you may need two cushions for double padding.

The Ideal Manager

There's often a big difference between what people think the ideal manager is and what he really is.

The ideal manager is no God—angel maybe, but no God. His goal is simple: help people exceed their expectations.

The ideal manager doesn't manage by crisis. He anticipates problems before they create a crisis.

The ideal manager doesn't need to take work home. He gets it done before the workday is over.

The ideal manager doesn't call and run meetings. His people do.

The ideal manager isn't a lecturer. But he is a teacher.

The ideal manager isn't drowning in any of his work. In fact, there aren't even any waves.

The ideal manager has things working so well that often he doesn't even need to manage.

The ideal manager has the emotional security and self-esteem to work himself out of a job.

The ideal manager may also be as rare as California condors.

Doing Whatever Is Necessary

In early 1982, Roger Straus III resigned as associate publisher of Harper & Row's trade book division. His job was one with an excellent salary and a lot of prestige. It was a job he enjoyed. So why did he quit?

As 1982's recession deepened, Harper & Row began to worry increasingly about their profit-and-loss statements. Executives decided that they needed to cut back on staff. They ordered Straus to cut back on his staff and budgets by "substantial amounts."

Straus reported in the July 19, 1982, *Wall Street Journal*, "I didn't quibble about the need for cuts. But we'd already gone through one staff reduction, and now I was being asked to cut out the muscle and nerve of the company, the $19,000-a-year copy editors who put out the books." How could he cut out the muscle and nerve of the company? He couldn't—and in the end he fired himself instead!

The productive manager is willing to do whatever is ethical, legal, and necessary to help the company meet its goals.

Too many managers follow their fears, doing only what they must, not what they ought. Fearing change, they may feel safe in maintaining the status quo. But they're safe only for today. When tomorrow's pressures descend, such managers won't be able to survive.

It's not always the manager who's at fault. Often it's the company itself. In many corporate atmospheres it isn't safe to say what needs to be said and to do what needs to be done. The result: The manager is pushed away from being productive. The door is closed.

When doors are closed like that, the company stagnates. *Whenever it's no longer safe to do the obvious, the people in the company are unable to reach their potential. And the company itself gets into the same fix.*

Sometimes the clear vision we claim to have is really obscured by our own ego.

I can see the problem clearly!

"Don't merely do your best; do whatever is necessary to get the job done."

Winston Churchill

Pulling Strings

President Dwight D. Eisenhower was a man with a broad leadership background. He had served for many years as an officer in the U.S. Army, eventually becoming one of the leading generals of World War II. He became a president of the United States, serving for two terms.

President Eisenhower made an effective demonstration of the art of leadership by using a simple piece of string. He would place the string on the table and say, "Pull the string, and it will follow you wherever you wish. Push it, and it will go nowhere at all. It's just that way when it comes to leading people."

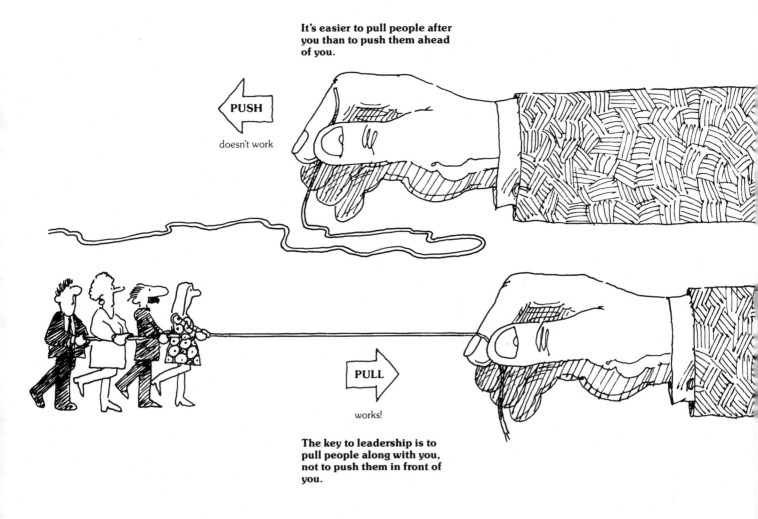

It's easier to pull people after you than to push them ahead of you.

PUSH

doesn't work

PULL

works!

The key to leadership is to pull people along with you, not to push them in front of you.

The Price of Leadership

Before you assume the position of leader, you had better ask yourself, "Am I willing to pay the price?"

OUR Hero

Productivity always involves some form of leadership: leadership in the marketing of tomatoes, the manufacturing of ball bearings, the innovation of dress design, or any other thing or service of economic value.

Leadership involves making choices, especially the hard personal ones. The following list contains things you are going to end up doing if you follow the road to a leadership position. Ask yourself if you are up to it.

• The buck passing inevitably ends up in your lap.

• Envious eyes are always watching you for mistakes, and they twinkle with glee when mistakes happen.

• No matter what you are involved in, between your position and others, there is a gap. You get lonely, so you force yourself across the gap, but problems are always the outcome.

• You are still at it when others say, "Good-bye. See you Monday."

• You get asked for more from those who don't know what it takes.

• You must see through the fog into tomorrow.

• There are teeth marks on your heels from the time the dogs got too close.

• You get asked questions you don't have the answers to, but everyone thinks you do.

• You are always fighting the battle between what you would like to do and what needs to be done.

• What you have struggled and fought for to obtain, others follow along behind and steal with ease.

Well, is leadership worth it?

If not, then think of the view you will have if you're not out in front.

Time Management for Managers

Time for Management

Time management is critical to any managerial success. At least that's the conventional wisdom of the day. Take a survey of managers at random, and you'll find they all agree: time management makes a difference.

"I feel like I'm constantly flooded with work. I know I could do better if I had better time management."

"Time management is better management."

"The manager who manages his time ends up with more time to manage."

That's the conventional wisdom. And there's a lot of merit in time management. But is it always the answer?

Sometimes the best way to manage time is to get rid of your workload. Get rid of the problem. Come up with free time. Then,

and only then, will you be able to accomplish all you'd like to.

How can that be done? Either totally eliminate the concern, or delegate it to someone else.

Examples:

• Marcus was concerned about his children drowning. He must have spent an hour a day chasing his kids away from the ditch that ran past their backyard. Finally he decided to get a grip on his time by eliminating the problem: he had the kids take swimming lessons.

Too often we have the image that being busy means we're good managers.

MR. IDEAL MANAGER

- Craig was a manager who didn't like to be tied to employees. He had a couple of eight-to-five workers, but they were always bothering him, asking, "What shall I do now, boss?"

  He never could get anything done because he had to keep his workers busy. Then he took the approach of freeing up his time: he fired the workers and began to use freelance help. (Not only did he free his time by eliminating a problem, but his productivity increased!)

- Harry enjoyed volunteer work, and he was good at it. But he was often overloaded—and enthusiastic helpers were constantly trying to take his assignments from him. He took the free-time approach and let them.

- Rhonda taught a class in design at a local college. By midsemester she was an appendage to the class because the students were teaching themselves. She found she didn't have to spend valuable time preparing for the class; the students did it for her!

- Allison was overloaded with work. Her assistant was busy too—but the assistant was willing to do extra in order to progress in the company. Allison let her, freeing up some of Allison's time.

The Value of the Free-Time Approach

It takes time to make free time. It takes more effort than maintaining the status quo. But once the approach has been put into effect, the free time starts:

You've eliminated the problem.

Or you've delegated it to someone else.

Most of us spend too much time managing other people's problems. But the free-time approach changes that. With the free-time approach we let others manage their own problems. We spend our time finding new people, new directions, new opportunities. And these new people and new opportunities become resources that will free up our time even more!

Hiring the Right People to Start With

Bosworth Company was in a hurry to get a new person. Their old marketing manager had quit, lured away by another offer, and they wanted to get a new one fast. The pressure the company was under was incredible. If they didn't get a new person right away, they could lose thousands in revenues.

The company president took over the problem personally. He interviewed the applicants, looked at their resumes—and made an offer within the week.

The new man looked like just what they wanted. His resume was very impressive. But after he'd been on the job for a few weeks, the president learned that appearances can deceive. He learned their new marketing manager had been fired from his previous job—for incompetence.

"If only I had taken more time," the president moaned. "If only I had checked his references. And talked to his previous boss."

But despite the new man's drawbacks, the president decided to work with him. He didn't want to go through the whole hiring process again.

We can solve a lot of problems before they become problems just by hiring right in the first place. It's much harder to get rid of an employee, even a new one, than it is to turn down an applicant for the job. Employees have allies in the company. They often belong to unions. They make their bosses feel responsible for the success of their lives. (Who wants to feel that he's put someone out into the cold?)

The answer is to hire the right people to begin with. When we pick better people we have fewer problems and greater contributions from each member of the staff.

Picking better people creates a better organization— whether it's the U.S. Army or a church choir.

Most enterprises need to spend more time and effort at the doorway, filtering out who gets in and who doesn't.

"Sorry, no!"

"Well, I'm ready for another day. Honk! Honk! Har-de-har-har!"

It is much easier to slam the door on the problem than to try and remove it once it has made itself at home.

The only clowns you want to see are in the circus.

People Filtering

Effective hiring is like putting people through a filter. A lot of people may apply to be hired, but you don't automatically let them into your company. Instead you put them through the filter. The filter should have several levels. On the first level you screen out a few applicants. On the second level you screen out a few more. And so on, until you end up with just the person you want.

It's amazing how little filters are used in some companies. What's even more amazing is that some companies delegate the hiring and firing of employees to a personnel department. "Here, Personnel Department," the manager says, "I'd like you to get me an employee that matches these qualifications." And the personnel department complies.

The problem is that so many subtleties are missed. Personnel departments can be useful—but use them only for the first, rough screening. Then the department doing the hiring can carefully check and recheck the applicants.

Get the Right Person

Use the right filters, and you'll solve many problems before they even get into your company. You'll get the right person for your job, rather than an incompetent.

Some filtering suggestions:

- Check references carefully. Talk to acquaintances of the applicant.

- Try to get a large quantity of people to pick from. The more people you interview, the more likely you'll get someone who's just right. Don't let time or your superiors pressure you into acting prematurely.

- Watch those first impressions. They can tell you a great deal.

- Avoid ideal job descriptions that only Superman would be able to fill (leaps tall buildings in a single bound). You'll get stuck looking for someone who doesn't exist.

- Write down the contributions you expect the person to make. Specify what it is that you need.

- Don't rely on a personnel department to find the person for you.

- Look for people in other areas and disciplines. A lot of great people are overlooked or ignored because they don't fit preconceived notions.

- Look for aptitude and potential, rather than specific skills. It's a rare bird indeed that comes to a new job and doesn't need additional training. Specific skills can be taught after the person is hired.

- Look carefully at the person's past performance. Chances are, if the person has done well in the past, he or she will do well for you.

- Look at outside interests. You probably don't want someone who is too narrow.

- Create a good test of the person's abilities, one that requires a chunk of time to complete. That will screen out the less interested applicants. At the same time, be flexible with the test. Some people will have legitimate reasons why they can't complete it all.

- Let others get involved in the hiring process. Make sure co-workers get a chance to have input. Some new employees fail because of personality conflicts with peers.

- Make sure the new employee knows what's expected. Too often it's just assumed the person knows what's needed and wanted—and too often that assumption is wrong.

- Ignore this whole list, and make one that will better reflect the uniqueness of your company and its people.

Picking good people is by far the hardest job any manager has to do. Once done, and done right, good people help the manager solve his other problems.

Miss Management

Judgment by Appearance

The board of directors met for a very important meeting. "We need to establish our criteria for our new CEO," said the chairman.

"Absolutely," said the older woman at his right.

"He should be articulate," said the red-headed man.

"He should be attractive. No one wants to work for someone who isn't pleasant to look at," said the man with the bow tie.

"He should talk tough," said the woman in the gray suit at the far end of the table.

"Okay," said the chairman.

They put out the word that they had an opening. Hundreds of highly qualified people applied. "Look at the incredible number of good people we have to choose from," the older woman said.

They began the interviewing and screening process. In came a man who had been executive vice-president of the number three company on *Fortune*'s 500. They looked him over carefully. "No, I'm sorry," said the red-headed man. "He just isn't articulate enough."

In came a disciplined entrepreneur who had taken three companies from zero status to net profits that exceeded a million dollars a year. "His credentials are excellent," said the man with the bow tie, "but he's not attractive enough."

In came the president of the world's largest conglomerate who wanted a job with a smaller company, something with less pressure. "He's articulate and attractive," said the gray-suited woman, "but he doesn't talk tough enough for my taste."

Finally the board found just the man they were looking for. He was articulate. He was attactive.

Too often people use the wrong criteria for evaluating others.

He talked tough. "Just what we wanted!" the board members exclaimed in unison.

There was only one problem: he didn't know how to lead. He didn't have what it takes to be a CEO. *His qualifications were only skin deep!*

Too often people use the wrong criteria for evaluating others. They act as though they're judging a personality or a beauty contest. Which seems to be the most articulate? Which is the most attractive? Which seems toughest?"

By using such criteria, those doing the evaluating may find someone who's articulate, attractive, and tough—but they have no assurance that they've found someone who can do the job! Here's how to avoid the pitfall: **Judge others by how they perform, not by how they look.** We shouldn't let appearances guide us. Instead, we should let the person's record speak.

Judgment by Sex and Race

Contribution is more important than gender or race or color or creed or education or age or anything *else*.

Unfortunately, that's not the way most managers operate. Instead of judging a person individually, they get hung up in their prejudices. They make stereotypical judgments for groups of people and let them apply to the individuals. Sometimes those judgments are positive, sometimes negative. But the fact remains: judgments of groups are never as valid as judgments of individuals.

By labeling people we restrict how we deal with them.

All too often our preconceived notions of what ought to be get in the way of what could be.

It's very useful to take time to account for how many tags we've stuck on other people—and on ourselves.

Here's an example. A Chicano is hired into a new company. Do they look at his qualifications? Do they look at his talents, his potential for growth? Not too closely, at least in this particular company. He's hired because "We're an equal opportunity employer!" He becomes the token Chicano.

But then things don't work out. Do they look at whether or not the man has been adequately instructed in his duties? Do they look to make sure they're using him for what he's best at? Do they offer him any sort of training to help develop his skills? Not in this company. Instead they judge him by a crude stereotyped view of his ethnic group: "He moved too slow. He was lazy," the personnel record says.

Another example. A woman progressed through the company she worked for until she became national sales director. She was incredibly effective—so much so that one day top management realized how powerful she was in the company. "We can't have this," they said. "She's a *woman!* Besides, she's *middle-aged!* We can't be in a position where we're reliant on a middle-aged woman!" So they restructured the company so that she'd have to move to a different city every four months. It was tough. And finally she did just what they'd hoped: she quit. She was fifty-five years old.

Too bad the company didn't know what they were letting go. Because this woman, named Mary Kay, had a double share of talent. She took $5,000 she had access to and started her own company, Mary Kay Cosmetics. In 1982 her company sold over $300 million in cosmetics.

There's only one valid criterion for judging people, and that's the contribution the individual can make. Everything else is relatively unimportant.

Judgment by Individual Contribution

When a manager judges an individual by his prejudices about a group, he'll get himself into a situation that wastes human talents.

- *Some* companies' only motive is profit. But *some* companies are also caring and humanitarian.

- *Some* Blacks can't play basketball. But *some* Blacks can.

- *Some* women make lousy managers. *Some* women make outstanding managers.

- *Some* people who talk slowly are stupid. But *some* people who talk slowly are careful thinkers.

- *Some* kids who act up are brats. But *some* kids who act up are simply bored.

- *Some* old people are senile. *Some* old people are more mentally alert than ever.

- *Some* kids are smarter than their parents. *Some* aren't.

When we need to judge someone, we should look at the individual. Look at that flesh-and-blood person, unique in all the universe. Then ask a very specific question: "What can this individual (fill in his name) contribute?"

Once we've learned the answer to that question, and only then, will we be in a position to act.

When the Boss's Baby Is an Ugly Brat

Beware of the baby trap! When you create something new in your job, it can become your own flesh and blood, and you can totally lose objectivity.

The boss comes in with a new idea. He tells the staff, "This is going to revolutionize the business."

"But, boss," one of the workers says, "that's just like the idea we tried two years ago—the one that failed so miserably."

"That's ridiculous," the boss snapped. "This idea is going to turn us right around."

So he pursues the idea. He builds on it. He pulls it close to his breast and won't let go.

When the idea finally fails, he just can't believe it. "It was my baby," he says. "How could it have gone wrong?"

It's easy to become emotionally attached to something we've originated. Whether it's an idea, a direction, a technique, a new product, a new employee, or something else, if we get too close to it, we'll lose objectivity. It will become our baby—and the person who attacks our baby had better beware!

We've got to keep our objectivity even about our own ideas if we're really going to revolutionize the business.

The Problem of Mother (or Father) Love

A university department head created an entirely new educational system. It was going to be the best thing in education since the classroom. Of course, the professor's idea had to be tested. So he began to gather data to see if it would work. Only one problem: his mind was so closed about his baby that he collected only data that supported his preconceptions.

Finally it was time to try the idea in the real world. The road was rough, but the professor struggled over every obstacle. He would listen to no disagreement.

Yet the approach failed miserably. "I can't believe the incompetence of others," the professor said. "If they had only done it right, my idea would be off and flying by now!"

When we get too attached to our children, we overlook their faults and failings. We fail to see how ugly they really are! If we're going to move ahead, we must learn to evaluate our brainchildren for what they are—sometimes worthless but once in a while truly good.

From the palace came an idea. It was a wonderful, marvelous idea—not because it was good, not because it worked, but because of who its owner was . . .

He uses a lot of superlatives in describing the baby.

He holds it up high.

He won't let the baby speak for itself.

He doesn't see how ugly it really is.

He holds it firmly in his grip.

He never lets anyone else hold it.

There are some key things that will help us identify that ugly brat as someone's favorite child.

Sometimes a child is born that has wondrous native beauty—and sometimes you'll have an idea that's truly fantastic!

Five Things to Do When the Boss's Baby Is an Ugly Brat

Nearly all of us face a time when the boss (or another worker) brings his new baby into the office. "Take a look at this," the boss says. "Isn't she a beauty? She'll solve all our problems. This is the greatest thing anyone has seen since the pharaohs built the pyramids!"

You take one look. It's the ugliest thing you've ever seen. "Hmmm," you say thoughtfully.

But you can't just leave it at that. Otherwise the boss will think you actually *like* his idea. Besides, what effect is the ugly brat going to have on the company?

So what do you do? Here are five suggestions:

1 Tell a Lie

One manager had the bright idea of saving money by forming a secretarial pool. Her assistant was given the challenge of organizing the pool.

The assistant knew it was a crummy idea. No one wanted to share a secretary. That was a blow to the ego, to a person's feeling of prestige. But the assistant knew the boss truly loved her new baby. So the assistant lied and told the boss he thought it was a great idea. Then the assistant did his best to implement the idea. All the while, though, he made sure everyone remembered whose idea it was. And when it ultimately failed, the assistant escaped unscathed. *

"That's the most beautiful and smartest kid I've ever seen."

2 Find a Few Good Points

The CEO of a small company was having trouble with his people filling out the proper forms. Because they were lax in filling out the forms, they also began to be lax in the actual work.

The CEO's solution: he created a checklist that every person was supposed to follow as he did the job.

"It fills up space in an interesting way."

The vice-president knew that solution wouldn't work. If people wouldn't fill out the form, they certainly wouldn't fill out the checklist. So the VP came up with an alternative solution: he pulled a few good points out of the checklist and turned them into a new company slogan. His approach worked, and he solved the company's problem. The VP applied the fine art of turning a sow's ear into a silk purse. And the pig didn't so much as squeal.

3 Tell the Truth

This approach is dangerous. We've all heard about the public official who spotted an error in the bureaucracy above him, and now he's working in a closet in north Alaska.

But telling the truth can work if you go about it right. One lady always told her boss the truth about his ideas, even if she feared it would rankle him. Gradually he grew to appreciate her. He now sees the wisdom of keeping her around as a debunker of stupid ideas. All new ideas now have to be run past this woman, who otherwise has little power in the company. But she can kill an ugly new brat with a simple curl of her lip.

"He's ugly and not too bright."

4 Don't Say or Do Anything

Sometimes the best thing you can do when you're faced with a foolish idea is *nothing*. A shipping department in one company is swamped with work—but their boss has little to do. So he constantly refines the process under which they work, sending out a flood of memos telling of his latest idea.

The department is too busy to mess with his ideas. They simply throw the memos into the garbage, then continue with their work. Everything runs well, and everyone is happy.

5 Modify It to Make It Work

"A possible job in a circus sideshow."

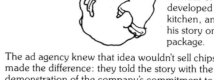

Some ideas are ugly babies as is, but a simple modification will make them beautiful. A potato chip company was beginning to break into the big time, and they hired an advertising agency to help them. The founder of the company had developed the chip in his kitchen, and he wanted to tell his story on the back of the package.

The ad agency knew that idea wouldn't sell chips. But a modification made the difference: they told the story with the right slant, using it as a demonstration of the company's commitment to quality and taste. The modification worked—the chips sold so well people couldn't eat just one!

*Beware of the Pinocchio syndrome. It is a common effect of this approach.

Seeing Reality behind the Shadows

Often when we get set on a course of action, we get so caught up in it that we fail to see the reality creeping up on us.

"Edsel is the car of the decade! We've designed for the future, and the future is here!"   Ford executive

"Carter will be known as one of the best presidents we've ever had. He'll win a second term in a landslide!"   Carter aide

"This is the world's first unsinkable ship!"
Designer of the *Titanic*

We laugh at these quotes, but the people who said them weren't just whistling in the dark. They had reason for being optimistic:

- **Marketing studies** indicated that the Edsel would be well received.

- **Preelection** polls showed that Carter would do well in his bid for a second term.

- **Mathematical models** of the *Titanic* and tests the designers and engineers conducted

showed that the ship truly was unsinkable. They just didn't pit it against a gigantic iceberg that would rip its side open.

So the Ford executive and the Carter aide and the *Titanic* designer all had something going for them. Where did they go wrong?

Seeing the Shadow, Not the Reality

The problem came when they put an overreliance on the numbers, the statistics, the models—and not on the reality.

- **The photograph** is not the actual object.

- **The graph** is not the exact position.

- **The paper money** is not the real value.

- **The reflection** is not the living person.

They all have a form similar to the reality, but they aren't the reality. They're simplistic, only suggesting the complexity that's really behind them. They're only shadows. You can learn a few things from shadows—but not everything there is to know about the real thing.

Those who follow shadows may end up in the dark.

"No, it's the Statue of Liberty!"

"Looks like an adult moose."

The shadows can get you in another way. I know of a credit union that for years tried to get its own building. It was associated with a university, but its bylaws said it was independent. They wanted to get off campus where they could exercise that independence.

So the credit union officials compiled a bunch of statistics showing how the union would grow too large for its quarters. "We need to move off campus where we'll have the room to grow."

The university said no.

The credit union compiled some more statistics, made some new projections. The university said no.

This went on for ten years. The credit union was trying to put its strength in its numbers, hoping they could give them the clout they needed. But this plan just wasn't working.

Finally one of the credit union workers suggested a new approach. "Let's see what the members want to do," he said. "And if they

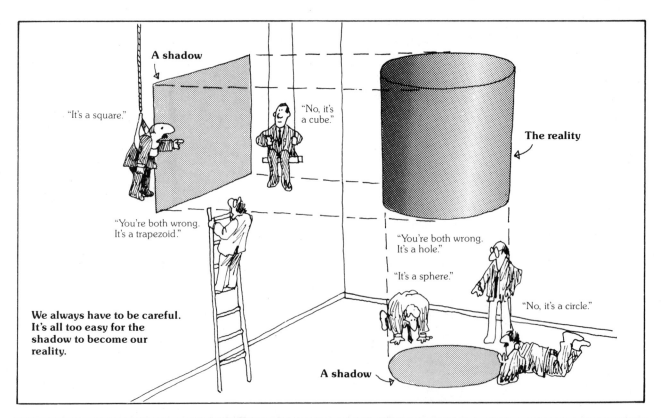

A shadow

"It's a square."

"No, it's a cube."

"You're both wrong. It's a trapezoid."

The reality

"You're both wrong. It's a hole."

"It's a sphere."

"No, it's a circle."

We always have to be careful. It's all too easy for the shadow to become our reality.

A shadow

want to move, as an independent body, we have the power to move."

They tried that approach—and very soon they were in a nice new building off campus. Once they stopped putting their hope in the shadow—statistics and projections—and put it into the desires of the people, they got what they wanted.

> **"The qualities that (scientists) measure may have as little relation to the world itself as a telephone number has to a subscriber."**
> Frank Rhodes

Following Shadows

Some time ago Penn Central Railroad was on the verge of bankruptcy. The U.S. government took a look and decided that the railroad's failing wouldn't be in the national interests. So they moved in to help the company recover. They gave them some money and sent some consultants to provide some much-needed expertise.

It didn't take the consultants long to discover one of the biggest problems: the company was collecting and working from too much data. It was set up to process and operate from an amazing mass of information. Instead of throwing light, the statistics cast shadows, and the shadows were putting everything in darkness. Company officials had no idea about what was really happening.

We don't have to live in a land of shadows. Help avoid it by

- **Looking** as closely as possible at the final reality
- **Refusing** to choose shadows over real things, people, or ideas
- **Going** to where that reality is, not allowing yourself to be separated by an abstraction

The True Source of Power

Most people who are at the top of their fields spend a lot of time out of the office. One important Japanese automotive firm insists that their designers spend three months selling cars in a showroom to give them a better feel for what customers want. And in one computer company, new vice-presidents are required to sell a computer system to a new client.

Such approaches are invaluable. They help the worker to see the reality, instead of just the shadow. The results do a great deal to strengthen both the worker and the company.

> **"American management decisions are based on statistical study of questionnaires and other data, while in Japan decisions are made on the basis of personal relationships and human considerations. The Japanese way is more realistic."**
> Noboru Terashima

"The map is not the territory."

Alfred Korzybski

Efficiency versus Effectiveness

Once I stood in a line at a fast-food place waiting my turn to order. The man in front of me placed his order, "I'd like a deluxe hamburger."

The teenaged girl had apparently been instructed to emphasize the correct name of the hamburger, so she said, "What *exactly* is it you would like, sir?"

"One of your deluxe hamburgers," the man repeated.

That was unacceptable to the girl. She wouldn't order the hamburger until the man named it correctly. And he didn't know the name she wanted.

In the end the man gave up and ordered a salad.

When the prime motive is efficiency rather than effectiveness, productivity will eventually drop. Both managers and workers will most likely end up being efficient at the wrong thing.

The result of seeking efficiency rather than effectiveness is getting caught in the activity trap:

- **Quantity rules:** The goal is more actions, more paper shuffled more times, more memos, more of anything you can see.

"I got a really great deal on last year's calendar!"

- **Activity dominates:** "If you ain't running, you ain't working."

- **Appearance controls:** "You looked great! Your work did too!"

"Nothing is more common than to find workers conscientiously and effectively performing unnecessary jobs. A well-run organization raises productivity by eliminating such jobs and reassigning the job-holders to needed work."
                                                    Robert Zager

Efficiency	Effectiveness
Asks how	Asks why and what
Goal: To improve the process or product	Goal: To determine the right direction
Objective: To have quantity and quality	Objective: To increase the value
"Everything is running well."	"What are we aiming for?"

Both approaches are needed, but the one on the right should dominate and come first.

Private Space

All animals, including humans, must have territory to call their own.

A Place to Nest

You've all seen the huge bay-type office. Government offices are good examples of what I'm talking about. The office is made up of one big room, with row upon row of drab metal desks.

When the boss comes out of *his* office, all he sees is a sea of humanity. There's no space for individuality in that kind of huge bay. It's difficult for the boss to identify with any one person. The workers have no identify, no place to call "mine." And they perform accordingly.

Then one of the workers gets a promotion. Raoul is moved out of the bay and into his own room. It's a place he can make fit with his personality. He moves from a space belonging to everybody jointly to a place he can control personally.

It's a great feeling. Raoul now feels more important, more needed, more vital to the organization. He's more willing to sacrifice for the company. He simply feels more a part of it. All that comes from just having a place to nest.

My Space or Their Space

Sometimes an individual space isn't enough, though. One company hired an interior designer to update its office building. The designers working for the firm put their stamp on everything in the building. A new secretary came in and was assigned her space. She had her own corner with her own desk, but it just wasn't her.

On the very first day she began a struggle to make the space feel like home to her. She put a small vase on the desk. She put some pictures of her family on the wall. She hung some quotations clipped from her favorite magazines.

Eventually she was able to feel more comfortable in her corner. But it was an uphill fight, from beginning to end. A tug-of-war occurred between this secretary and the interior designers. Everyday the feeling of the office sapped some of her energy simply because *someone else* had imposed their feeling, their personality on her little space.

Everybody Needs It

Birds need a nest. It is vital to the continuation of their species, and if they don't have one, they'll try to build one or move elsewhere to find one.

People are no different. We need a place too. If we can't get it at work, we'll try to change the circumstances at work. But if that isn't effective, before long we'll leave, looking for a new nest where we are comfortable and can be productive.

Every bird needs a place to call his own.

31

Shared Desks

See if this sounds familiar. A company had so much work to be done that it couldn't house all the workers. There was only one solution—management decided to put everyone on split shift. One crew would come in early in the morning, work at their desks, and leave in the afternoon. Then the second crew came in. They'd work at the same desks and leave later in the evening.

Not surprisingly, employee turnover increased drastically. But production didn't.

Then the company reorganized its work space. And even though it decreased the space allotted to each worker, it did provide each with his own little nook undisturbed by others. Immediately turnover decreased.

Everyone needs a home at work. Everyone needs a room, a desk, a space that's theirs. It needs to be a little corner of the world that they can call their own and stamp with their own personality.

With Territory Comes Responsibility

A neighbor bought a watch dog (if you could call him that) to watch over his home. He is the kind of dog that looks like a moving mop with two beady eyes, but he does guard the house. He considers the house his, and he watches over it with a vengeance. When you pass through the gate, he suddenly appears, yipping at your heels, and then when you go back out of the gate, he disappears. The house and yard are his. The little dog is responsible for protecting it.

Now the point is not that you want your workers attacking your customers; obviously you don't. The point is that if you give your workers their own territory, they'll feel responsible for their performance in the same way the dog did.

How do you give each worker his own space in a way that promotes productivity? Here are some ideas.

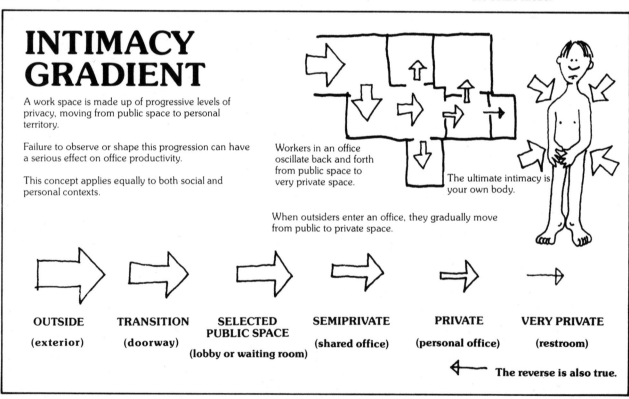

INTIMACY GRADIENT

A work space is made up of progressive levels of privacy, moving from public space to personal territory.

Failure to observe or shape this progression can have a serious effect on office productivity.

This concept applies equally to both social and personal contexts.

Workers in an office oscillate back and forth from public space to very private space.

The ultimate intimacy is your own body.

When outsiders enter an office, they gradually move from public to private space.

OUTSIDE	TRANSITION	SELECTED PUBLIC SPACE	SEMIPRIVATE	PRIVATE	VERY PRIVATE
(exterior)	(doorway)	(lobby or waiting room)	(shared office)	(personal office)	(restroom)

The reverse is also true.

Intimacy gradient is an idea taken from *A Pattern Language* by Christopher Alexander, Oxford University Press.

The Opportunity to Fail

Being in a box gives a certain security. But it does limit growth and movement.

Everyone has a habit of keeping other people in boxes. Others do it to us; we do it to others; we do it to ourselves.

It's not very comfortable in a box. So why do we let ourselves be boxed in?

We fear if we don't, we'll end up too involved in too many things, stretching ourselves so thin that we'll fail.

But there's a real drawback. When we're in a box, we don't replenish ourselves. Every box has a leak somewhere. And we may not only lose opportunities but also lose what we already have.

The amount of success any person achieves is generally proportional to the amount of risk he takes.

An old saying puts it very well: "Nothing ventured, nothing gained." How about this one: "The turtle never makes any progress until he sticks his neck out." Or this: "You have to give your life away to find it."

Fearing Failure, Loving Success

If we spend our lives fearing failure, we'll end up spending our lives failing. Only by jumping out of the box that limits us and going for the risk will we be able to get to where we want to be. We have to give ourselves—and others—the opportunity to fail.

Mickey Mantle was one of the greatest baseball players of all time, noted for his incredible ability to hit home runs. But look at his record:

536 home runs   1,710 strikeouts   1,734 walks

3,444 times at bat without getting a base hit tells us he hit the ball less than half the time. His career batting average of .298 equals a cumulative total of going for seven years without hitting the ball!

Abraham Lincoln is one of the most beloved presidents in U.S. history. But he gave himself the opportunity to fail. Look at his record:

1831—failed in business

1833—defeated in bid for legislature

1833—again failed in business

1836—suffered a nervous breakdown

1838—defeated for Speaker of the House

1840—defeated for elector

1843—defeated for House of Representatives

1848—defeated for House of Representatives

1855—defeated for Senate

1856—defeated for vice-president

1858—defeated for Senate

1860—elected president

Before you put yourself, or anyone else, into a safe little box, remember this: the opportunity to fail is inseparably linked to the possibility of success. If you can't give yourself the first, you won't be able to get the second.

"No man is truly free who is not permitted occasionally to be irresponsible; nor is any institution."
Tom Wicker

Givers and Takers

There are two kinds of people we all have to work with: the givers and the takers.

Givers

raise up

smile a lot

"Others need this."

build good relationships

look to the future

promote financial well-being

"What can I do?"

find success

make up twenty percent or less of the population

Takers

pull down

frown a lot

"I desire that."

build poor relationships

regret the past

increase financial troubles

"What can you do?"

catch a lot of problems

make up eighty percent or more of the population

Givers are productive. They produce what's needed. They bring profit to the company they're associated with. They fill you up. Givers have high self-esteem.

Takers are unproductive. They take rather than give. They are a liability to their company. They suck you dry. Takers have low self-esteem.

Party Poopers and Party Givers

Overheard at a party: "I always like to come here to Jane's house for parties. They're always so fun. She has everything you need for a great time." *Jane is a giver.*

Overheard at another party: "I thought I was going to have such a great time here at Martin's tonight. I don't understand why I feel so bad." *Martin is a taker.*

The Emotional Bottomless Pit

Mike is a bureaucrat's bureaucrat. He has file cabinets spilling out of his office and running down the hallway. He likes to drop in on his fellow workers, just for a little chat. He has a constant flurry of paper flying from his office into every other office in the company.

Mike is a taker, not a giver. He squanders space, resources, and time—both his own and everyone else's. He spends his time and energy, not for results, but to fill up some emotional bottomless pit. He's concerned with his own selfish needs, rather than the needs of the company or the people around him.

'Tis Better to Give than to Take

Productivity comes from avoiding takers and low self-esteem and concentrating on givers and high self-esteem.

Here's a key: Even though a person may generally be a giver, if he takes in the one area that's critical to the company's success, he'll suck you dry. And even though a person may generally be a taker, if he gives in the one area that's critical to the company's success, he'll fill you up.

Note: The more power and control you give to a giver, the more he'll give back. The more you give a taker, the more he takes.

There may be said to be two classes of people in the world: those who constantly divide the people of the world into two classes and those who do not.

Benchley's Distinction

Producers and Consumers

Producers versus Consumers

Henry was a great entrepreneur. He was skilled both in investments and in business management. He dabbled around in different businesses, making money in them all, looking for the kind of business he would most enjoy.

When Henry was forty-five, he found his life's love: the car dealership business. He started a new company and quickly became one of his area's most successful car dealers. When Henry died, he left behind him a dealership worth several million dollars. His heirs were pleased, to say the least.

Henry's daughter Terri took over the management of the business. Things went well for several months. Then Terri hired her cousin Rob to be the company accountant. Terri brought in her uncle Bill to be vice-president, a position Henry had thought unnecessary. Terri invited an old family friend, Ahmad, to become the vice-president in charge of sales, and Ahmad was happy to accept.

Terri's management decisions seemed to be just what the company needed to move to a new level of sales. But any advances they made were only temporary. The company began a long decline, as Terri and her relatives and friends in management sucked it dry. Finally the company went bankrupt.

The problem with Terri's auto dealership was that it had too many people consuming the proceeds of the company and not enough producing them. **The productivity of a company increases as the number of producers goes up and the number of consumers goes down.** On the other hand, as the number of consumers goes up in proportion to the number of producers, the productivity of the company will decrease.

All organizations will have both producers and consumers, and both are necessary. The key is to have the proper balance—the more producers, the better.

Consumers—

- Maintain the organization itself
- Give the others the opportunity to produce
- Do *not* relate directly to the product or the service; do not directly bring value from the customer
- Serve as:
  managers
  controllers
  secretaries
  lawyers
  accountants
  chairmen
  principals

relate to maintenance and control

Producers—

- Give direct value to the company
- Create the product; perform the service
- Often serve as:
  salespeople
  repairmen
  teachers
  installers
  assembly workers
  engineers
  designers
  ditchdiggers
  innovators
  line workers
  waiters

relate to the creation of the product or service

the people that create a customer

The optimal situation occurs when all the people are doing something all the time that directly brings a profit, when all are producers. Of course, the optimal often isn't realistic—managers, secretaries, and accountants are important and necessary, but

---

Note: This chapter may upset a few people, and some of them may be very productive. But I've found that most managers confuse production with consuming. The functions of maintaining, protecting, and recording the work of the company don't produce income for most companies. Yet those functions take up most of the time and payroll.

they're often not as necessary as we think they are. Productivity can go nowhere but up when we place the emphasis on producing people, rather than on consuming people.

The Problem of Imbalance

We can see how deadly a producer-consumer imbalance can be when we look at our current Social Security system. When the system was devised, it seemed like a good idea. There were millions of workers, and just a few of those would be retiring every year. It would be easy for the workers to pay for the "old-age insurance" of the others.

But over the years, the population mix has shifted. In 1940, there were eight-and-a-half workers for every retired person. In 1980, there were only about five workers for every retired person. And in 2030, experts project that there will be only two-and-a-half workers for each retired person.

Suddenly it becomes evident that the system doesn't work. The ratio of producers to consumers must be very high, or any organization will collapse under its own weight.

The Social Security system shows us how vital it is that there be many producers for each consumer.

Our Greatest Resource

People are our greatest resource. They're also our greatest drag. It all depends on how we use them. If we want to move to new levels of success and productivity, we need to release our people to be producers, rather than consumers.

That's not always easy. Our society has a bias toward making people consumers. But if we want to survive, we've got to resist that pull.

If we let the consumer side of our organizations proliferate, the whole thing will eventually collapse.

Get the consumers off the producers' backs: an idea that will work productive miracles.

The Imbalance That Threatens Social Security

Workers per Retiree

1940

1960

1980

2000

2020

2030

The number of people twenty to sixty-four years old per person sixty-five and over.

From Social Security Administration, Federal Reserve Bank of Boston

---

We need to release our producers to produce.

Too Many Chiefs

The Corpse of Engineers

"I once worked with the Corps of Engineers on one of their projects. They called me in to meet with their job managers. I visited with one after another. I couldn't believe how many chiefs they had, and how few braves! With all those chiefs, I spent time

- In meetings
- Filling out reports
- Taking their calls
- Answering their correspondence
- Gathering in conference with them

"And still we hadn't gotten any work done!

"Finally we got the project moving. But when it got right down to doing the work, the chiefs were nowhere to be seen. Only four of us were left, and two of us were graduate students.

"It was hard to finish the project because all these chiefy fingers kept reaching down into our pie. But finally we were able to complete the job, and I moved on to other things."

Too many cooks spoil the broth. And too many chiefs hinder the work of the braves. In fact, **the greater the number of managers in proportion to the number of employees, the less productive the company will be.**

With too many chiefs, a company will have too many telling and too few doing. And if too few are doing, too little will get done.

"Since you're our last brave, a lot depends on you!"

37

Excellence

"An excellent plumber is infinitely more admirable than an incompetent philosopher. The society which scorns excellence in plumbing because plumbing is a humble activity and tolerates shoddiness in philosophy because it is an exalted activity will have neither good plumbing nor good philosophy. Neither its pipes nor its theories will hold water."

John W. Gardner

Give Him a Little Praise

"My man has fleas!"

Give him a little praise, and he'll do anything.

An old dog trainer once had an interview on national television. He was a crusty old gentleman, a little brusque with people, but he sure knew his dogs. He'd won just about every prize in the book, and now he was sharing his secrets with the world.

"When you have problems with a dog, what kind of punishment do you use?" the interviewer asked.

"I usually don't have problems," the trainer answered. "And I very seldom need to punish."

"So how do you train the dogs?"

"It's surprising what a pat on the head will do," came the answer. "Dogs are very much like people—they'll do just about anything for a little praise."

Building Self-Esteem

When Gene married Ellie, he had no idea that she suffered from low self-esteem. But he found out soon enough. She felt that she wasn't worth much. It deeply troubled her.

But she found a way to feel better. She began to tear others down. If she could find others' failings, she'd feel like maybe she wasn't so bad after all.

"She saw everything as a threat," Gene explained. "Every situation in her life, including the things *I* said and did, were viewed as attacks on her self-image."

Shortly after they were married, Gene decided he needed to do something to change Ellie's outlook. He began to look for every opportunity he could to build her self-esteem. Several times a day he praised her for something she'd done, or for just being her:

"Ellie, your hair sure looks nice today."

"You look fantastic in that dress!"

"Your macaroni and cheese has to be the best in the world."

"Thanks for keeping the house so clean."

"Mrs. Keller was telling me how much she appreciated your help at the school program last week."

Gene's effort took years. But gradually Ellie changed. Now she's a different woman. She feels good about herself now. And she feels good about her relationship with others.

People need to be recognized as being of value to others. We will do whatever is necessary in order to receive that recognition.

To take the idea one step further: when we receive recognition, a little praise, we're much more apt to do what other people need.

Recognition can come in many forms: money, words, attention, medals, gifts, promotions, public announcements. Money is perhaps the most often used in business situations. It's often not the money the person wants, however; it's what the money communicates: that the person is of value.

The Case of the Persecuted Manager

Wally was branch manager of a bank. He enjoyed that kind of work, but he sure didn't like his job. It didn't matter what he tried, he'd still catch heck from one direction or another.

If he made one person happy, he'd ruin another's whole life.

The customers were rude.

The employees didn't like his decisions.

His bosses were always on his back.

Pressure, pressure, pressure. Wally began to feel like a failure. He started to get ulcers, and they started to grow bigger and bigger.

Finally he turned in his resignation.

The people he worked with were astonished. "How can you quit?" they asked. "You're the best we've ever worked with."

The customers told him they wished he'd stay.

The employees told him they didn't know how he could be replaced.

His bosses told him they'd do whatever they could to keep him on.

But by then it was too late. Wally had suffered for years without any praise, without any positive feedback. He decided to stick by his decision to leave. And the company lost in more ways than one.

When Wally left, the new man took over. He was less experienced. He didn't have the education and know-how. Overall, he was much less qualified. And he came on for more money than Wally had made after all those years.

It's too bad that no one recognized the problem earlier. The whole situation could have been saved with just a little praise.

How to Do It

Praise and recognition are easy to give. After all, they're such little things! But they need to be given in the right way. Praise given grudgingly isn't going to be very well received. Recognition given at the same time as criticism is ill timed.

Here are some ways to make praise most effective:

- Tie it to performance, not to a schedule.
- Give it often.
- When it's deserved, give it quickly.
- Give it sincerely. If you can't praise in a sincere manner, don't say anything.
- Give it consistently. If two people do well at the same thing, praise them both. If people do something well more than once, praise them as many times as necessary.

"The success of IBM's sales and service force, Tupperware's distributorships, and Frito-Lay's sales force depends largely on the recognition their management lavishes on them."

Unknown

Watering Weeds or Rewarding Right

"If I were a first grader in one of the suburban schools, I would conclude that schools are geared toward two important things: lining up for lunch and putting the chairs on the desks at the end of the school day. These are the only two things that every teacher I observed adamantly insisted on. The child can only conclude that these tasks—and not reading—are terribly important. Everything else in the classroom is more or less laissez-faire. All sorts of distractions are allowed."

Bruno Bettelheim

• Why are levels of competency in reading, 'riting, and 'rithmetic falling year after year? Perhaps because we're rewarding the children for learning other things, such as lining up for lunch!

• Why is productivity down on the production line? Perhaps because we're rewarding the worker for things other than production—for orderliness, perhaps, or following company policy.

• Why are we suffocating under an avalanche of paper? Perhaps because we're rewarding middle-level workers for producing that avalanche! It's not uncommon for a white-collar worker to be evaluated according to how much paper crosses his desk. And because of that, it's to be expected that he produces and processes ever-increasing amounts of PAPER.

Whenever a manager is having trouble getting his desired results, the problem may be in his reward system. **Often managers unknowingly reward for the opposite of what they actually want.** He may be watering weeds instead of vegetables—and in business, as in farming, you get what you water.

No matter what your intention, if you water and fertilize weeds, you get weeds!

"I'm very disappointed in you, Harold. Your productivity just has to improve."

How to Water Right

Neither managers nor farmers want weeds. When they water them, it's strictly by mistake. But it is possible to water right so that the desirable characteristics of employees will flourish and their undesirable ones will shrivel and die.

Here's the key: People are attracted to things they're rewarded for. They're repelled from the things they're punished for. That's simple and obvious—but too often forgotten. Whenever we want people to do more of something, we should give them rewards. Whenever we want them to stop, we should punish them.

People are repelled from things they're punished for.

People are attracted to things they're rewarded for.

That sounds simple enough. But one person's reward is another's punishment. Everyone's perception is different. A manager may think he's punishing when the recipient views it as a reward.

Whether something is a reward or a punishment depends on the perceptions in the person's mind.

"One man's carrot is another man's stick. And an allergy to carrots or a tendency to masochism complicates things further."
Fred Yates

How We Usually Water

• Seven-year-old Ricky wants some attention. Daddy's reading the paper. Ricky pesters and pesters, whines, fusses, kicks the cat, and knocks over the piano bench. Finally Daddy's had enough. "That's enough," he says, and he sets about to punish Ricky for his misbehavior. Over Daddy's legs Ricky goes, fanny up. Swat! Swat! Ricky cries, runs from the room. "That will teach him," Daddy mutters to himself.

But twenty minutes later, Ricky's doing the very same thing again. Why? Because Daddy *rewarded* him for it!

• Alex can't stay out of prison for more than three months. Once he's behind bars, he's lost his freedom: He can't go on a trip or go to the shopping mall or go to the bar or go to the races at the speedway. He rarely gets to see his wife, and she's about ready to file for divorce. The chow in prison is lousy. He doesn't much like the job they give him to do, although it's better than nothing. Alex doesn't even like crime!

There's only one thing that keeps him going back to prison: The other prisoners give him a powerful reward. They respect Alex. They treat him like the patriarch, the grand old man of the prison. And that reward makes up for all the drawbacks of prison life.

Alex would rather be in jail than anywhere else. Why? Because he's a hero there.

• Karen believes visibility is the key to success in her company. She reasons, "How can you climb the promotion ladder when it's locked in another room?" The answer: get into the room where the ladder is. Because of that, Karen does whatever she can to get into the big boss's office. Karen doesn't think her supervisor has much clout. It's the manager of the whole department who has the power.

Whatever Karen does, she does it big. Often she has fantastic ideas, so when she succeeds, she succeeds in a big way, and the manager calls her in to compliment her personally. But equally as often Karen has harebrained ideas that she blindly pushes through against all advice from her colleagues and supervisor. So when she fails, she does it big, and the manager calls her in on the carpet.

But calling Karen in on the carpet doesn't deter her from railroading through her ugly brainchild the next time—that's partly what the manager has been rewarding her for!

The Question

One man's punch is another man's poison. The first questions to ask about any person one hopes to motivate are these: *What does he consider a reward? What does he consider a punishment?*

Once those questions are answered as accurately as possible, you'll be ready for the next questions: *What are the consequences of my performing the way I have? How should I change my behavior if I hope to motivate others to improve?*

Time for Action

Once those questions are asked and answered, you'll be ready to move into action. Follow through—consistently—on what you decided.

Don't fall into the trap of giving out medals for bad work, no matter what form the medals

come in. Don't make the mistake of rewarding people for doing the things you hate.

A Little Help

So how do we turn the waterspout in the right direction? Borrowing a page from child psychology will help. These ideas will work for adults as well as kids:

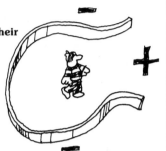

Kids typically go energetically in all directions. Channeling their behavior by rewarding only the good actions increases the chance of having a productive adult.

If the person is involved in negative behavior, but it's not dangerous, ignore him. **Do absolutely nothing!**

Determine to give no rewards whatsoever, except for positive behavior.

When the person does exhibit positive behavior, give a reward as soon as possible. That will reinforce in his mind the connection between the behavior and the reward.

Give rewards for positive behavior often. And remember that rewards can come in many forms. For a child, for example, you may give a smile, an encouraging word, praise, a hug, a treat, time together, and so forth.

A draftsman in one company was a big problem. When he wasn't complaining about problems, he was causing them. The management bent over backward to accommodate him, but it didn't do any good.

Then they decided to stop watering their weeds. They began to ignore his complaining and problem-causing and instead rewarded him for the things he did well. He quickly began to improve.

In your desire to water wisely, don't make the mistake of failing to water at all. A plant that doesn't get any water (or light or fertilizer) will die.

Note: This approach doesn't work with everybody. Many people do what they please, no matter what managers and supervisors above them do or don't do. (See "Manipulation Won't Work.") But in spite of that, it still is surprising how much lousy behavior is actually encouraged by management.

Manipulation Won't Work

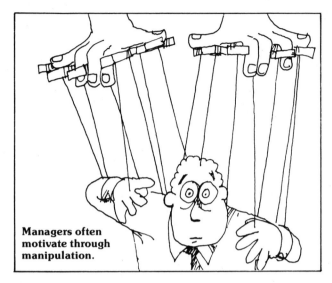

Managers often motivate through manipulation.

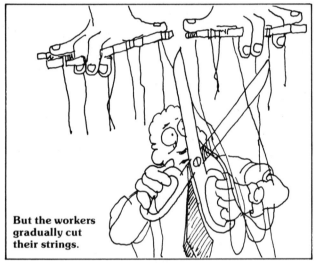

But the workers gradually cut their strings.

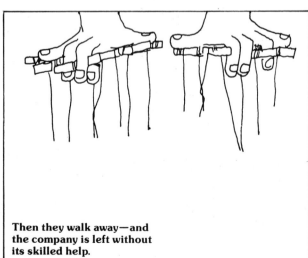

Then they walk away—and the company is left without its skilled help.

A manager can't consistently control the behavior of another person by manipulation. He can try all he wants, of course. He can threaten, coerce, bribe, beg, challenge, swear, or whatever he wants to do. But over a period of time, he's probably going to end up doing exactly what he pleases.*

Be a Doctor, Not a Sleazy Businessman!

I know of a young man whose mom wanted him to be a doctor. All through school she encouraged him—to the point of even doing his homework for him. When he had a hard time in college, when he was tired of studying, when he wanted to go out on a date instead of doing his homework—his mom would fill in for him. How could he ever be a doctor if he didn't get good grades in college? And how could he ever get good grades if he didn't do his homework? And if he wasn't going to do his homework—well, she'd do it for him!

He passed through college with good grades. He applied to medical school and was accepted. When his school year started, he moved to the city where his new school was. He started attending classes. But some nights he just wasn't in the mood to study. Some nights he decided he'd rather go out on a date.

By the end of the first semester he was put on academic probation. By the end of the first year he flunked out.

His mother was devastated. But the young man wasn't. He went on to become a very successful businessman—which was *exactly* what he'd wanted to do all the time.

We can be like the mother and drag a person a long way to get them to do what we want. But in the end they'll likely do precisely what *they* want and nothing else.

"Manipulation, regimentation, coercion, for whatever motive or reason, will ultimately fail to produce good results."

Dean Larsen

---

*The best way to encourage workers toward positive behavior is the wise and consistent use of rewards. See "Watering Weeds or Rewarding Right." However, not even this approach will work with all people.

Why People Aren't Responsible

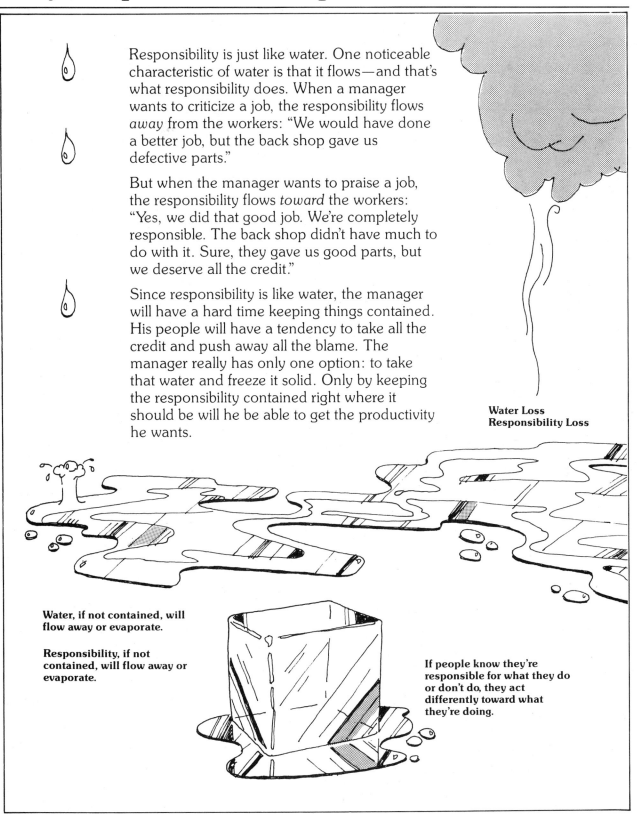

Responsibility is just like water. One noticeable characteristic of water is that it flows—and that's what responsibility does. When a manager wants to criticize a job, the responsibility flows *away* from the workers: "We would have done a better job, but the back shop gave us defective parts."

But when the manager wants to praise a job, the responsibility flows *toward* the workers: "Yes, we did that good job. We're completely responsible. The back shop didn't have much to do with it. Sure, they gave us good parts, but we deserve all the credit."

Since responsibility is like water, the manager will have a hard time keeping things contained. His people will have a tendency to take all the credit and push away all the blame. The manager really has only one option: to take that water and freeze it solid. Only by keeping the responsibility contained right where it should be will he be able to get the productivity he wants.

Water Loss
Responsibility Loss

Water, if not contained, will flow away or evaporate.

Responsibility, if not contained, will flow away or evaporate.

If people know they're responsible for what they do or don't do, they act differently toward what they're doing.

He Did It, Not Me!

I have a batch of kids at home. One day they were playing in the bathtub during their bath (these are *little* kids), and someone splashed water onto the floor. Not just a few drops—the floor was so covered that it seeped through the cracks at the side of the floor and started to drip down into the basement. Dad was in the basement. Guess who got his head wet? Guess who got mad?

I stomped up the stairs and put towels around the kids and lined them up. "All right! Who splashed the water?"

"Not me!" they chorused—and the bigger kids pushed the smaller ones in front of them. The results were going to be negative, and the responsibility flowed to the weakest.

Another day one of the kids surprised me by cleaning the house. I called them all into the living room. "Who did such a good job cleaning?" I asked.

The kids sensed a reward coming. "I did!" everyone said in unison, and the big kids pushed the smaller ones behind them. The responsibility had flowed to the strongest.

(Luckily, I happen to be the usual kind of father. I *knew* who had splashed the water and who had cleaned the house.)

Take Credit; Give Blame

There's a sad story about an up-and-coming electronics company. They abused the flow of responsibility. Whenever there was a success, the guys in the front office took responsibility: "We did it!"

Whenever there was a failure, the front office passed the responsibility on: "The engineering department is responsible!"

Unfortunately for the company, all the good engineers left. And everything went downhill from there.

Take Blame; Give Credit

On the other hand, we can look at the success of Bell Labs. They know the properties of responsibility, and they use them properly. They put responsibility where it truly belongs, whether the results are good or bad, whether credit belongs up front or in the back shop.

Because of this, the labs have prospered. Their developments range from fiber optics to semiconductors. Some of their personnel have even received Nobel Prizes for their work.

Success comes to those who keep responsibility contained. Credit goes where credit is due; so does blame. When responsibilities are delegated, they stay where they've been put. The liquid isn't allowed to drip away. People seem to be more willing—even eager—to work under these conditions. They know they'll get what they have coming, whether it's glory or pain.

When there's blame, people move back. When there's credit, they step forward.

To be fully productive, people have to take responsibility.

Cutting Out the Hierarchy Distance

"I sure hope all he wants us to kiss today is his deskpad."

It seems to be human nature: As soon as a certain kind of person gets a little authority, he starts to flaunt it. One day he's one of the guys; the next day, with his new promotion, suddenly he's a king and you're the slave. There's suddenly a great distance between him and the rest of the workers.

I'm Superior

I taught at a university for a while, and my boss there was the perfect embodiment of what I'm talking about. He was a small man, overly round. Somewhere he picked up a Napoleon complex. He was always strutting around, sticking his nose into everyone else's business, forcing his way in, finding ways to get more authority over more people.

His game was to win, no matter what. He thoroughly dominated those under him. They either knuckled under or quit. There was no middle ground.

And, oh yes, he was a success! You could tell it by the way he lorded it over his underlings. He rose to great heights in the university. But his success was built on the resentments of others.

The Sony plant in San Diego has only one lunchroom. Managers and factory workers eat there together. It has no reserved parking spaces. Even top managers must come early to get a good space.

That boss taught me an important lesson: **The greater the distance between the manager and his workers, the less natural cohesion there'll be in the organization.**

Natural versus Forced Cohesion

If the people unify naturally (and it can happen), a company will really be successful. But when there's distance between the boss and his people, that natural unity won't come. He'll need to force unity. And that works only on the surface.

If a boss is acting high and mighty, do you think his workers will help him out? No way! They'll say, "If he's so great, he doesn't need our help!" Success goes out the window.

Cohesion and Productivity

Japan is one of the most productive countries in the world, and the Japanese companies, government, and employees are unified in their goal of productivity. A survey by the Organization for Economic Cooperation and Development gives the answer: Japan is *the* country in all the world that has the least difference between the highest and lowest incomes.

The countries of South and Central America are among the least productive in the world.

Many of those countries suffer from constant upheaval. One possible explanation is that there is a wide economic gulf between the haves and have nots.

An Expensive Belief

Those who believe they're superior have to pay a high price for it. They fatten their egos at the expense of others—who are probably starving. And when the superiority complex shows up in a company, that attitude can overshadow everything else.

For three decades Ho Chi Minh withstood the mighty assaults of three nations, two of them superpowers. How did he hold his small forces together? As Jules Roy described it in his book, *The Battle of Dienbienphu,* "There is nothing to distinguish their generals from their private soldiers except the star they wear on their collars. Their uniform is cut out of the same material, they wear the same boots, their cork helmets are identical and their colonels go on foot like privates. They live on rice they carry on them, on the tubers they pull out of the forest earth, on the fish they catch and on the water of the mountain streams. No beautiful secretaries, no pre-packaged rations, no cars or fluttering pennants . . . no military bands. But victory, damn it, victory!"

Distance can take many forms. Read on for more talk about distance.

- **Physical distances**
- **Social norms**
- **Prerequisites**

- **Locations**
- **Salaries**
- **Qualifications**

- **Status**
- **Beliefs**
- **Anything of value to both people**

Cutting Out the Operations Distance

Too Big for Their Own Good

"I long for when our company was small," says a company president. "Things were better then. We have a metal-working company, and small seems better. When we got government contracts, especially with the Pentagon, suddenly we were too big for our own good.

"Now we have all kinds of new departments and branches in other cities. I'm afraid the distance from me to my managers, both here at headquarters and in the other cities, is too great. We've lost touch. I feel I've lost some control.

"But the worst part of all comes when you look at the bottom line: our profits per job were better then than they are now!"

The greater the distance between the various elements in an organization, the greater the problems tend to be. And the more resources are needed to solve them.

The Dangers of Distance

- The Miller family is separated by work. They live in Detroit, where the wife works. The husband works in California; he flies home on weekends. The distance increases their expenses dramatically; it has also created serious family problems. In fact, the family is on the verge of shattering.

- Studies have shown that obese people, who have grown too large, live shorter lives. Perhaps it's because the distance from one point to another within their bodies has grown too large. Blood vessels and nerves, bones and muscles are asked to bear more than they're capable of.

- Power companies have learned that the longer the distance they have to transmit the power, the greater potential line loss. By

Distance is a relative term, depending on what you're comparing to what.

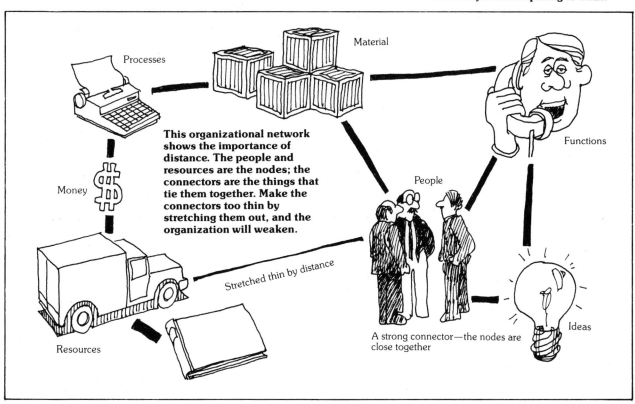

Processes   Material   Functions

Money

This organizational network shows the importance of distance. The people and resources are the nodes; the connectors are the things that tie them together. Make the connectors too thin by stretching them out, and the organization will weaken.

People

Stretched thin by distance

Resources

A strong connector—the nodes are close together

Ideas

shortening the distances, they're able to eliminate a lot of problems.

- As a company grows, it adds more and more layers of management. Soon there is an uncomfortable distance from one level to the next. The costs of communicating within the company rise dramatically, both in a fiscal and in a personal sense. Misunderstandings increase.

Cut the Distance

There's only one solution to the distance problem: cut it out! Cut out the amount of distance there is between levels within your company. And cut out the distance between points of operation.

Some approaches:

- Communicate on a one-to-one basis, and communicate directly to the people who need to hear the message. This is far and away the best way. Anything else is only second best—or worse. Play the game of Gossip for a few minutes, passing a message from one person to another till finally the tenth person in line gets it. How distorted is the message by that point?

- Move resources closer to where they're needed. The Japanese have an effective approach called "just in time." With "just in time," they specify that their suppliers deliver the needed material just in time for it to be put on the production line. Their subcontractors are to do their work just in time for it to fit in with the work of others.

- Shift the power to decide. Let the person who must execute the work decide how it should be done. For instance, the secretary types the letters. Let her decide what format to use.

- Let the company grow like a living thing. Living things don't grow to infinite sizes. Each has an optimum size—and each has a maximum. Once the company has reached

its mature size, don't let it grow anymore. Let further expansion take other forms; for example, let the company reproduce, creating new offspring. For more on this, see "Three Ways to Grow."

Tighten Up the Distance

Consider the war of the future as an analogy. If we got into a world war at this point (God forbid!), we wouldn't fight it the way we have in the past. Instead of transporting troops to meet on some battlefield, our generals would most likely wage the war with small, highly mobile weapons operated by computers from their own bunkers. To do otherwise would mean immediate defeat: with the distances involved and with today's sophisticated weaponry, by the time messages were sent and received, the battle would be over.

The same applies to businesses. As distances grow and as technology continues to develop, communication becomes more and more crucial. The manager who doesn't conquer the distance problem will end up sending messages to workers who made a different decision an hour before. And the battle will be lost.

The closer you are, the easier it is to relate.

Burp!

Choosing Who Makes the Choices

"A few days before Christmas, a railroad official called the Chicago office of United Parcel Service of America Inc. and confessed that a flatcar carrying two UPS trailers had unaccountably been left on a siding in the middle of Illinois. UPS is no Santa Claus, but it tries its best to deliver Christmas packages on time. So the regional manager paid for a high-speed diesel that whipped the flatcar into Chicago ahead of an Amtrak passenger train, and he ordered two of UPS's fleet of 24 Boeing 727s diverted to Chicago to get the contents of the trailers to their destinations in Florida and Louisiana in time for Christmas. In spite of the extraordinary expense, the manager neither asked permission nor even informed UPS headquarters in Greenwich, Conn., until weeks later.

"'We applauded it when we heard about it,' says Kent C. Nelson, UPS vice-president for customer service. 'We give these guys complete authority to run their operations and do their jobs. We push decision-making down to the lowest possible levels.'" *from Business Week*

Productivity can be increased by putting the decision-making powers as close as possible to where the effects of the decision will be felt.

A few examples:

- If the decision on new equipment will affect the workers on the assembly line, let them make the decision themselves.

- If the decision on classroom policies will affect the teacher in the classroom, let him make it.

- If the decision on modification of the new product will affect the salespeople, let them make it.

- If the decision on customer relations will affect the clerk at the counter, let her make it.

- If the decision on the copy machine will affect the repairman, let him make it.

Cut Out Management

One major insurance company decided it needed to cut back on some of its employees so that the profits could go up. The common approach is to cut back on the work force and to leave management alone. But this insurance company decided to do it the other way around: they cut out management and left their workers alone. Their profits increased, just as they had hoped!

It's a sign of inefficiency when all the decision-making power resides at the upper levels of the company.

The Manager's Credo

In one business, the top three people were always very busy working—but not with the business.

The president was usually busy with his golf game.

The first vice-president was busy with the new business he was trying to get going on the side.

The second vice-president was busy trying to get her master's degree.

One of the office workers for the business had a good question: "Why doesn't the owner just get rid of them and let us do their work. We're doing it anyway!"

Probably the worker was right. The three managers weren't contributing, but at least they weren't meddling destructively. In fact, they were following the Manager's Credo: "Why solve someone else's headache when they can do it themselves?"

With their managers gone all the time, the workers in that company had learned to make all the decisions themselves. They did a good job of it, too. Despite the absentee managers, the company maintained its position in the marketplace and continued to be successful.

"I'm too busy. You solve the problem. Tell me what happened after I get back from playing golf."

Trusted Assistants

Frank is a very successful college football coach. He's a good example of letting other people do the managing. Picture this scene: It's toward the end of the fourth quarter, and the score is tied. The camera scans over to Frank. There he stands, hands in pockets, casually chewing gum. What's he doing? Is he worried about his team? Is he getting ready to give orders to his quarterback? No—he's standing there watching the TV camera crew!

"By the time we get to the game," Frank says, "my job is over. At that point I may as well trust my assistants and my players."

Frank must be doing something right in his managing: his team consistently wins their conference, and they're consistently ranked in the top twenty nationwide.

This kind of system takes a fair amount of time to set up. It means that the manager must coordinate with his people; he must plan company strategy carefully; he must train his workers to do excellent work; he must take pains to communicate the underlying philosophy that drives the company.

But once he's laid that groundwork, he can step out of the picture, at least to a degree. He can give the power to make decisions to his subordinates and let them do things on their own. If the foundation he's laid is firm, the subordinates will make the right decisions.

How to Transfer Management

This may sound a bit radical, but in one sense the goal of managers should be to work themselves out of a job. They should be willing to let go of the reins enough to allow their workers to succeed without them. That kind of

management by absence can be surprisingly effective.

Our society seems to have developed an obsessive belief that things need to be managed from above. But often they can be managed just as well on the actual level of the work.

That doesn't mean a manager must give up control of everything. He or she should maintain control of who has what responsibility. He or she should maintain control of the information the staff works from.

But the manager's most critical function is **finding stuff.** And that's where a manager can most productively spend his time. He can most benefit his company by finding the right

- People
- Knowledge
- Opportunities
- Resources
- Capital

Controlling the finding, but not the people, is the essence of true productivity. A recent study showed that most managers spend only 8 percent of their time on analysis, contemplation, problem solving, and conceptualization. Yet that's where they should be spending most of their time, if they hope to be effective finders.

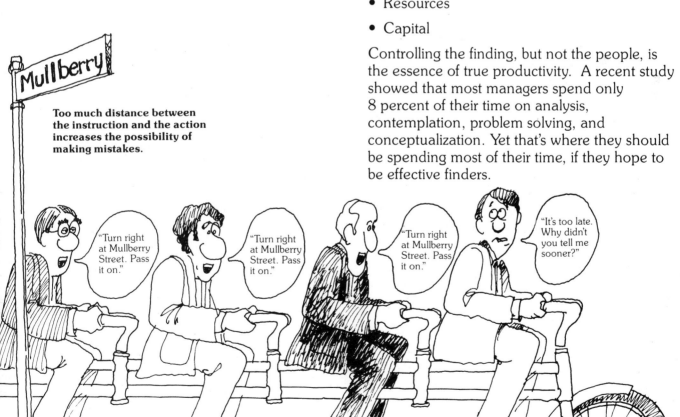

Too much distance between the instruction and the action increases the possibility of making mistakes.

"Turn right at Mullberry Street. Pass it on."

"Turn right at Mullberry Street. Pass it on."

"Turn right at Mullberry Street. Pass it on."

"It's too late. Why didn't you tell me sooner?"

Are You Holding Your People Back?

Barriers are set up to be hurdled. Ceilings are built to become floors. Walls can turn into doors.

Our greatest barriers are the ones we impose on ourselves and others.

Let me explain what I mean. For decades the four-minute mile was a barrier that couldn't be broken. If a runner mentioned his goal of breaking the record and running a mile faster than four minutes, he'd be laughed at.

But all records exist to be broken. And British doctor Roger Bannister decided he'd break this one. He'd been a world-class runner for quite some time, so his body was in good condition. Now he decided he'd condition his mind. For months he worked on his attitude, on his self-belief. Others said it couldn't be done. But Bannister had a different view. He felt that it could—and that once the barrier was broken by one person, many would be able to break it.

On May 6, 1954, Dr. Roger Bannister ran the first mile in less than four minutes. In just four years after that time, the four-minute mile was broken forty-six more times! And now all kinds of runners can do the mile that fast.

The Great Holdup

What's holding us back? What's keeping us from reaching our full potential, both as individuals and as companies? **Our biggest problem is often the fact that we set up too many barriers in our mind.** We see the four-minute mile and think the barrier can never be broken. We see a certain level of production and think that's the best our people will ever be able to do. We see a certain level of performance in ourselves and feel we're doing our very best.

These attitudes are hard to get rid of. They're sometimes part of our very being, and we're not quite sure we can shake them. But shake them we must if we hope to change and improve.

Today's Self-imposed Walls

Look at some of the barriers we've constructed in our present society. Plan on every one of them being torn down:

- **"People will always need gas stations."** But as electrical battery power improves more and more, the day may well come when we're all able to keep our cars running without gas.

- **"There will always be a need for printers."** Yet already electronic media are threatening the printing industry. The time may not be far distant when "copy" is transmitted directly over the wire into every home.

- **"We need supermarkets."** Some forecasters are talking about a new system by which food is ordered through our TV-computer hookups.

- **"Our nation is built on steel."** If a stronger and cheaper material were found, steel would find itself out in the dirt. We already have a stronger metal—titanium, which has one-fourth the weight and four times the strength of steel. If experts were able to make it cheaper, well . . .

- **"Democracy will reign forever."** Until times become so bad that the economy collapses and we're all deluded by a charismatic new messiah.

- **"A computer will never replace my job."** In reality, many professional workers can expect to be among tomorrow's unemployed—unless they plan ahead.

- **"The book will always be around."** Yes, and so will the hand-set printing press! A computer the size of a book is around the technological corner, and it will have the power and software to contain a small library. The bookshelf may have to go.

- **"Science will never create life artificially."** Maybe not this year, but wait till you read the Nobel Prize nominee list for 1999.

The only way any organization will ever be able to survive is to climb over the barriers that are set up around it. Change is continual—and inevitable. Managers can work toward controlling it—or can let it control them.

"It is by the process of constantly pressing upon one's limits that life gets larger."
Arthur E. Morgan

The Manager's Guide to Performance Appraisal and Job Requirements

Job requirements are usually created in one of three ways:

1. Pull the job requirements out of the air.

2. Bat ideas around with peers, and then commit them to paper.

3. Assign the job to a steering committee. (The committee will dutifully produce pages of trivia that are often irrelevant to the real situation.)

Those who are successful in business, however, use a different approach. They base their criteria for job success on real-life situations. **They evaluate the performance of people who are actually in the job in question and then define the job accordingly.** By finding a living, breathing person who meets the criteria they have in mind, they know that their ideals are humanly possible.

"Cheer up! Next year you may be able to measure up."

Performance	Far Exceeds Job Requirements	Exceeds Job Requirements
Quality	Leaps tall buildings with a single bound.	Must take running start to leap over tall buildings.
Timeliness	Is faster than a speeding bullet.	Is as fast as a speeding bullet.
Initiative	Is stronger than a locomotive.	Is stronger than a bull elephant.
Adaptability	Walks on water consistently.	Walks on water in emergencies.
Communication	Talks with God.	Talks with angels.

Note: I would like to give credit to the person who created the above chart, but I've been unable to track him or her down.

High Flyers

One company set up a training program for pilots. As part of their effort, the company wanted to be certain they had the best possible criteria for evaluating their graduates. They went to the best pilots in the business and found out what they could do—and what they were able to do when they had first learned to fly. This simple approach to establishing standards soon made the company's program one of the most respected in the country.

On the other hand, a friend once went to a local business to apply for a job. She filled out the forms and had the interviews. Then the employer gave her the list of qualifications he required—it went on for nearly ten pages. "No one on earth could have met those qualifications," she lamented later. And perhaps she was right: two years later the job opening was still unfilled.

The problem, of course, is that the business had unrealistic demands. They had created a description of the ideal employee—but the employee was so ideal that he or she didn't even exist.

This chart shows the requirements for a simple job in a major corporation. It's really just a bit of nonsense, but some descriptions of job requirements are about this ridiculous.

Meets Job Requirements	Needs Some Improvement	Does Not Meet Minimum Requirements
Can leap over short buildings only.	Crashes into buildings when attempting to jump them.	Cannot recognize buildings at all.
Not quite as fast as a speeding bullet.	Would you believe a slow bullet?	Wounds self with bullets when attempting to shoot.
Is stronger than a bull.	Shoots the bull.	Smells like a bull.
Washes with water.	Drinks water.	Passes water in emergencies.
Talks to himself.	Argues with himself.	Loses these arguments.

A Lot of Talk

Communication is a vital key to productivity. If a manager can effectively convey to his workers just what it is he wants, he's much more likely to be able to get it.

More than seventy percent of our time is spent in some form of communication. If we'd become better at it, we'd find our overall productivity increasing accordingly.

I've had experience in the past with all kinds of communication, from newsletters to films to speeches to museums to books. Over the years I've learned two important things about communication:

1. Communication is critical. When it's effective, it enables an individual or organization to get what is wanted.

2. Most communication fails.

My examination of the principles of communication showed me what works and what doesn't—and why. I began to apply what I'd learned, and the difference between before and after was very noticeable. It was so noticeable, in fact, that people would come up to me and ask how I did it. "That was one of the most effective presentations I've ever seen. How do you do it?"

Here is my answer to that question. These ideas, when applied, will do wonders for the productivity of any organization. No longer will the channels of communication be muddy. No longer will people fail because "I didn't really know what you wanted me to do."

Most communication is built on the wrong assumptions. It can be successful only when it's based on correct principles.

Obvious but Effective

I suspect that these ideas are so basic they're often overlooked. In fact, the ideas are so obvious that many people don't try to apply them even when they've been called to their attention.

"What's your approach?" they ask.

I tell them.

"Oh, that's obvious," they say. And then they continue to do what they've always done.

Yet the difference between the false assumptions and correct principles is as great as night and day. The ideas work for all kinds of communication, big or small, formal or informal. Give them a try. You'll soon be a believer!

Only when we move from false assumptions to correct principles will we become truly effective in communicating with others.

False Assumptions	Correct Principles
Information has an inherent value.	Information is valuable only when the audience or receiver so determines.
The goal of any communication is to send information.	The goal of communication is to cause change.
Communication best flows from the communicator to the receiver or audience (top down).	Communication best flows from the receiver to the communicator (bottom up).
Communication is a desirable end in itself.	Communication is only a means to an end.
Success is measured by whether the message was heard, the time was spent well, the money spent was worth it, and so forth.	Success is measured by comparing the results wanted with the results obtained.
The meaning is in the media.	Meaning is found in the receiver.

Any simple idea will be worded in the most complicated way.
Malek's Law

Walking in Another's Shoes

Some people give lip service to getting into another's shoes. But they don't even know how to do it, and they don't learn anything from their pseudo-empathy.

To learn from another, you must actually put yourself into his or her situation.

Each person wears a different kind of shoe.

The more you understand another person's point of view, the more you'll be able to reach him. Only when you've reached him will you be able to influence him.

Pseudo-Empathy Made Easy

Here's a typical way of showing empathy. We're overhearing a conversation between a manager and secretary:

Manager: You don't seem to be your naturally happy self lately. What can I do to help?

Secretary: I'm having a few problems at home. But it's getting a lot better.

Manager: Well, good. I know what you really need in your office: a change. We'll redecorate it.

Secretary: Oh, it's just fine. I have everything organized, and the file . . .

Manager: A bold new carpet, a better desk, and—about that chair, didn't you bring that from home? You shouldn't have done that. We'll buy you a new one.

Secretary: But it works just fine, and I'm . . .

Manager: Rather than wait, let's do it now. Let's move your desk over there. Grab hold.

Secretary: Ah! Ah! . . . My back isn't quite over the operation, and the desk is okay here. I like . . .

Manager: Just grab there on the side. We'll have it moved in a jiffy.

Secretary: Grunt . . .

The kind of empathy shown here is the usual kind we see. Really, it's not empathy at all. It's pseudo-empathy, where one person *pretends* he understands the other. Usually the pretense is only on the surface; just below the skin the manager doesn't want to be bothered with how the secretary really feels.

Getting a Different Point of View

Getting into another's shoes can give you a whole new perspective. I once worked with a loan manager who sat behind her desk all day, every day, giving loan interviews—for four years. Then she and her husband decided to buy a house, and it was her turn to be interviewed for a loan. She came back from the interview looking frazzled. She had obviously been perspiring heavily.

"You look like you've been through the wringer," I said. "What happened?"

"I had no idea a loan interview was like that," she responded. "The pressure is tremendous. It's one of the worst things I've ever experienced!"

Julie sees the need for better communication between departments.

Alvin sees the year's profit picture.

Roy sees the trouble he's having with Dave.

Dave sees the problem with the computer.

Ann sees her way as the only way.

Different people have different points of view. The manager won't be completely effective until he knows what makes each of his people tick.

Couldn't See the Crumbs

I have several kids, and they all have gone through a messy stage where they spill their food all over the table. To help them learn better, I have them pick it all up.

One day one of my kids did a pretty poor job. "Pick up that last piece," I ordered. He looked bewildered. "Right there," I said pointing. He looked around but acted like he couldn't see it.

Finally, exasperated, I got down on the floor beside him to stick his nose in it. Surprise! From that viewpoint I couldn't see the food either! It could only be seen from three feet above the table. It's funny how we always think others see what we see.

I didn't make the effort to see what he saw.

Party Pooper

One woman in an office couldn't be pleased with any party we ever had. No matter what we tried, she would complain. Either the food wouldn't be to her liking, or the time, or the place, or the activities. So one day I decided to put her in charge of our upcoming party.

She was thrilled. "Great," she said. "Now we'll have something good for a change."

But she came back a week later. "I can't do this," she said. "I try to have roast beef, and half the people complain because they want ham. I try to have it by the pool, and half the people protest. I just can't win. Please give the assignment to someone else. I promise I'll be happy with whatever they plan."

Getting into someone else's shoes has great power. This woman finally saw what things were like from the *planning* side of the party!

To Get Empathy, Try This:

- **Put Your Ego on the Shelf.** It's natural to insert your opinion into everything you experience, whether you express it vocally or not. Try to resist that. Try to be objective, to stand back, to feel what the other person is feeling. To do that, you need to pretend that you really don't care what you are feeling.

- **Make Empathy a Central Goal.** Always have it in the back of your mind that you want to feel what they feel, see what they see, think what they think. If you don't *plan* to feel empathy, you never will.

- **Set a Schedule.** Seriously. Select regular times when you'll seek to empathize with those around you. Those will be times when you'll *consciously* put yourself in their shoes. Don't try it too often—it can be a very draining experience—but do try it regularly and consistently. You'll be surprised at how effective it can be.

- **Try Their Job for One Day.** If you can't do that, try about half a day or at least an hour. This can be the biggest eye opener of all. More insight can be gained from a few minutes spent there than years looking from the position you're in now. You would probably rather not be bothered, but can you afford losing that insight?

Some managers genuinely want to be more empathetic, but they don't know how to go about it. For them, the exercises above should provide a start.

Blind for a Day

One morning I decided to try an experiment. I put on some dark glasses that completely shielded my eyes; they made me utterly unable to see. I stumbled through the house, trying to accomplish the simplest tasks in my blind state:

I went to get a drink of water and turned the tap onto my sleeve.

I went to the refrigerator for a snack and by accident got the mustard instead of the jelly. My peanut butter sandwich didn't taste too good.

I wanted to read but couldn't.

I wanted to watch TV but couldn't follow the story without the pictures.

I tried to put a record on the stereo but couldn't tell which album was which.

In the end, I just sat in the middle of the living room floor, discouraged. Since that morning I've never thought of the handicapped in the same way again.

Another day I decided to take a nap. One child had already fallen asleep on my bed, and I didn't want to disturb her, so I lay on another child's bed. It was horrible! I shifted and turned, but no matter how I lay, the springs and the mattress conspired against my back. This child had complained about his bed, but his troubles never sank in. Now they did; suddenly I understood!

Wearing Shoes

If productivity in your company isn't up to par, it may be that your workers' shoes are too tight. Or too loose. Or too new or too old. It's easy to prescribe what the problem is and what the solution should be. But chances are you'll be wrong.

The manager does just about all his work through others. The more he knows about their situation, their problems and concerns, the more he'll be able to help them in meaningful ways.

An old European proverb says, "Don't try to judge another man until you've walked for a mile in his shoes." That's a good tip for managers. And if you find you don't like the shoes you're walking in, you may come to understand why that particular worker isn't doing all he should.

Why Others See Things So Differently

Two presentations on the same topic:

The first was short and to the point. The speaker was dressed in his shirt sleeves. He quickly sketched his ideas on the chalkboard, then sat down.

The second took more time. The speaker was dressed in a three-piece suit. He used visual aids and handouts.

The material in the first presentation was more accurate. But the people believed the second presentation more.

Why?

Because people usually have the opinion that the more effort the speaker expends, the more value the presentation has. They look through the window of that belief; it affects the way they respond to everything they see and hear.

The only way to get through to a person is through his or her window. If the listener believes that money is the measure of success, then the speaker had better consider that bias when he prepares his communication. If the listener believes that all Asians are

Everyone has a window he or she looks through.

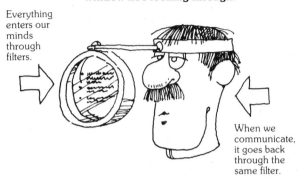

What a person sees in a presentation depends on the window he's looking through.

Everything enters our minds through filters.

When we communicate, it goes back through the same filter.

superintelligent, then the speaker should keep that in mind as he speaks. If the listener believes that all women should stay in the home or that a college degree can make a manager out of mincemeat or that we're drowning in a paper explosion, the speaker should remember the "window to the world" that the listener has.

A window is not universally real, of course. But it is real to the person who has it:

- It is a personal construction, built from past experience, training, and the personality of the person who has it.

- It gives the person a unique view of the world—and dictates how that person reacts to the world.

• If the communication coming in to the person doesn't match the window, it won't get through or it will be distorted.

Organizations look through their windows too.

• Even organizations have windows, and they use them the same way individuals do.

Sometimes a window can give a false view of reality. For instance, when the U.S. air traffic controllers went on strike in the early 1980s, they did so because their windows told them

• The financial loss of a strike would be worth it.

• Their employers would fold under the pressure and allow them the additional benefits they sought.

• They were irreplaceable.

But the windows gave them a false picture. Instead of getting raises, the strikers lost their jobs. Eventually, even their union folded.

" I once worked with a businessman on a consulting basis. He was tough to work with—it was like we lived in two different worlds. I tried one approach with him and failed. I tried another. Failed.

"But finally I found out what made him tick. His attitude was 'Because of my experience and success, all decisions are best made by me.'

"How could I work with that? I realized that if I were to get anywhere at all with him, I'd have to manipulate him into thinking the decisions I was making were being made by him.

"But in taking that approach, I would be at the same time decreasing my value to the organization. It would look like I wasn't making any contributions—he was doing it all.

"It was a tough double-bind, and there was no way past it. In the end I had only one course I could take—I had to leave. All because of the manager's unique perceptions."

John Marlowe
Business Consultant

"I'm a freelance editor who once worked full time for a book-publishing firm. Recently I returned to that company to help them on a special project. I couldn't believe their perceptions and the basis of their judgments. It was as if they put on blinders before making any decisions.

"But what bothered me even more was the fact that I used to wear the same blinders. I used to look at things in the same way they do."

Lanny Hobson
Book Editor

As you deal with other people's windows, look out. You have one too, coloring and filtering what you see!

An improvement in productivity begins with self-assessment and exploration of assumptions—looking at what is written on the window.

How to Get Through the Window

If we hope to be able to get through someone else's window so that we can enlist their help in accomplishing our goals, we first have to know what the window is. Then we can deal with it. To find out what someone's window is,

• **Ask for their opinions.** Find out their attitudes, feelings, ideas, beliefs about how things should be. Discover their pet peeves, expectations, predictions, anticipations, past successes and failures.

• **State until they agree.** The way to make sure you understand someone is to repeat back their words and feelings until they agree that you understand them. Everyone loves to be listened to—and an open ear can tell you a lot about a person.

• **Look for patterns.** Watch the choices people make. They reflect the beliefs people hold dear. The kind of car they buy, the friends they have, the color of clothes they wear, all are outward expressions of inner beliefs.

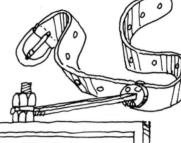

A given person's window is often filled with inconsistencies.

I should manipulate my employer to get the most I can for the least amount of effort I can put out.

You get out of this life what you put into it.

My employer is a generous person.

Honesty is the best policy.

Written on each individual's window are some belief concepts through which they view the world. If you find two of these concepts that conflict, you have a disharmony. If you can provide a route out of this conflict, change can be the positive result of this disharmony.

If you're having a problem dealing with another person, you may want to try to get him to change his window. The best way is to show a conflict between two beliefs. **Find two beliefs that are inconsistent; then get him to see the conflict between the two.**

For example, one person may believe that you should get all you can from your employer, regardless of the means. He may also say that honesty is the best policy. That's a point of conflict. You can help him see that inconsistency by posing a question about the differing beliefs. As he answers it, he'll have to deal with the problem.

Or you may want to diagram the opposition on a piece of paper or chalkboard. I've consistently had great success with this approach.

Human beings have an inner desire for consistency. They'll strive for it and do all they can to achieve it. If you can show the inconsistency, the other person will generally do what's necessary to correct the situation.

"A human being always acts and feels and performs in accordance with what he imagines to be true about himself and his environment [his window]. This is a basic and fundamental law of the mind. It is the way we are built."
Dr. Maxwell Maltz

The Pressure Dynamic

It's a high-pressure world out there, especially in business. We all feel the squeeze that comes from

- The high cost of the money that's needed

- The lack of qualified people

- Ever-encroaching deadlines

- Increasingly effective competition

- And on and on!

The usual response to pressure is to pass it on to someone else. **When people get under pressure, the release tends to happen at the weakest point.**

A simple experiment will show you about pressure and release at the weakest point.

- **The boss** yells at dad at work. Dad comes home and yells at the kids. The kids kick the dog. The dog turns around and bites the cat. Everyone's under pressure—and they seek a release by mistreating someone or something they see as weaker than they.

Whenever people get under tension, they seek a release through someone weaker than they.

- **Lava** will seek the weakest rock fracture lines through which to push to the surface.

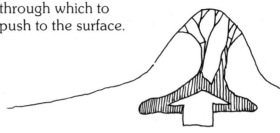

- **A man** gets malaria. After a long bout he recovers. But in his weakened condition the malaria returns.

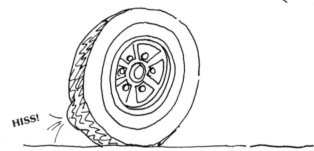

HISS!

- **A car tire** gets more and more worn. The pressure is great. Finally it blows—through the weakest point.

- **One of your employees** may be one of the mainstays of the company. It doesn't matter what you ask him—he always comes through. But then he starts to slip up. He forgets things. He messes up with key accounts.

What's the problem? Look at his pressures: he's going through a divorce; his mother's sick; his dad just died. No wonder he's not producing up to snuff!

Pressure is necessary. If we didn't have it, nothing would ever happen. We'd sit around fat and lazy.

But when it becomes too great, something needs to be changed before we blow.

If the pressures in your shop or company are too great, productivity is definitely going to suffer. What can you do?

A Few Suggestions

1. Find a release—let some off. You've all met Mrs. Indispensable. She's in charge of her department, and *nothing* gets done without her. Her work is her life. The company grows, and her department along with it—and her workload along with that. Still she hangs on, trying to do it all. But the pressure's killing. The answer: Mrs. Indispensable has got to find a release. She's got to delegate some of her duties. Only that way will she be able to survive without blowing.

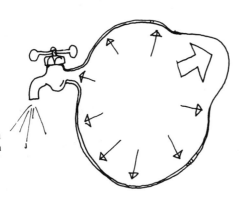

When the pressure gets too great, you need to find a good point of release.

2. Reinforce the weak point—strengthen it. One employee's weak point was the clock. Whenever he had a deadline, he'd freeze up. The quicker he needed to have a project done, the more time he'd take on it. His frustration would prohibit him from performing the way he needed to. "The hurrieder he went, the behinder he got." The answer: His boss saw the weak point and took steps to strengthen it. He set a time limit for the employee. "Do the best you can within the time limit," he said. "If you don't get done, that's okay. I'll take responsibility."

The boss's involvement removed the pressure. Suddenly the employee was able to perform better.

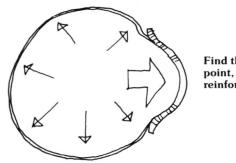

Find the weak point, and give it reinforcement.

3. Rechannel the pressure—find a new path for it. One company I know of puts its workers, both management and labor, under extreme pressure. One of the vice-presidents almost buckled under it. He was very aggressive, and he reacted aggressively. Things came to a head when he came about one inch from having a fistfight with another vice-president. He knew he was ready to blow—he had to find another way to release the pressure.

His answer: he took up contact karate.

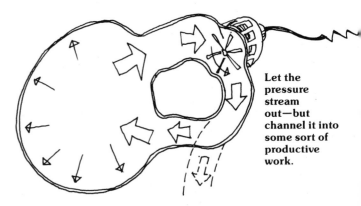

Let the pressure stream out—but channel it into some sort of productive work.

Keep an eye on the people you're responsible for. If someone seems to be under too much pressure, help him find relief—or productivity will suffer.

Note: Different people respond differently to different kinds of pressure. What to some may be a crushing blow may motivate others to rise to new heights of achievement.

Keep It Simple

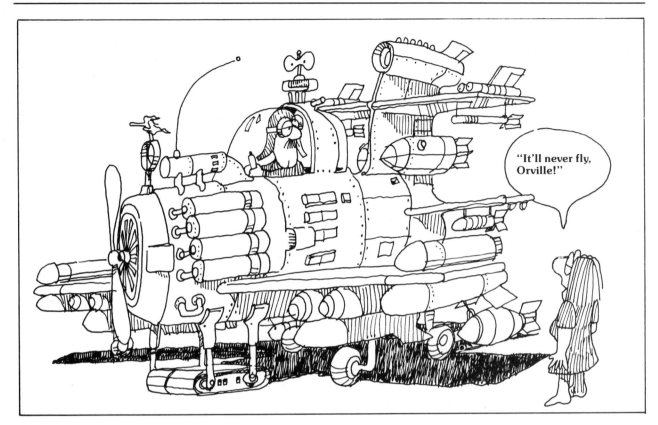

"It'll never fly, Orville!"

Simple or Complex

When business computers were first becoming popular, Luther decided his company should have one. He went out shopping and found out what was available, compared different models, and finally made his selection.

"It was one of the dumbest decisions I've ever made," Luther says. "We got a unit that was too complicated. It was way too much for what we needed. It took up too much space. We should have gone simple, but instead we went complicated. If only I'd have gotten a minicomputer! It would have cost a fraction as much and still have done everything we needed."

Luther's mistake is a common one. It stems from a tendency we all have: we tend to get more complex than we need to. **But only by keeping things simple can we keep things well managed and under control.**

Evidence of the Human Tendency to Complicate Things Is All Around:

- First we were able to buy a radio all by itself. Then they combined it with a tape recorder. Then they put a record turntable with the combination. Add on external speakers. Throw in a blender and a toaster. Good luck fixing it if anything goes wrong!

- The Pentagon used to make tanks for a few thousand dollars. But they've complicated them and now costs are sky high.

- Penn Central and W. T. Grant and Company were forced out of business. The key factor in their failure: unmanageable complexity.

- Even Betty's Soup Kitchen has had problems: Betty started putting new and unusual ingredients into her soup! The trouble was the new ingredients were expensive; the soup took longer to fix; and the soup didn't taste as good as it used to!

Successful Companies Do It

A recent study of some of the world's most successful companies reached some interesting conclusions. As a company grows larger, the general tendency is to let it grow more complex. *But the most successful companies resist that tendency.* They have only a few goals, and they often emphasize only one business value.

IBM has grown into a giant. Their products are complicated, but the company's goals remain simple. By having a clear, undeviating vision of their goals, IBM has been able to remain a world leader.

McDonald's has enjoyed similar success. The huge chain was one of the pioneers of the fast-food business—and they still manage to hold back the competition. How do they do it? They've remained true to their original goals and values.

McDonald's and IBM, as well as the thirty-five other major companies in the McKinsey and Company study, all have one thing in common: simplicity.

Just because a company grows larger doesn't mean it has to become more complex. In fact, in terms of individual involvement, the larger company can be *less* complicated. Here's how:

In the small business, the manager has to do a wide variety of tasks. As Theodore Leavitt explains it, "The owner-manager of a small variety store with some 3,000 stockkeeping units . . . has a far more difficult and demanding task than the head of K-Mart with his 1,492 stores. The owner-manager has to do everything, including the bookkeeping, purchasing, selling, repairs, even janitoring. The head of K-Mart does none of these. Division heads and department heads under him each do only one of these tasks. Their job may be big, but it's relatively simple compared with the owner-manager's. By subdividing work, K-Mart has become simpler, more manageable, and thus bigger."

Simplicity need not be sacrificed to growth. In fact, simplicity can promote growth.

We Can Do It

We can counter the tendency to complicate. The answer is to make a conscious and constant effort to simplify at every level of our business. But simple isn't necessarily easy. Often it's more difficult to simplify things than it is to let them grow complicated. Simplification so often goes against our natures.

But simplification will come with effort, and the results of that effort are worth it. Some ideas:

- Have one prime goal in the business. More than that will complicate things and diffuse your effort. As a senior executive of one of the companies in the McKinsey study said, "More than two objectives is no objective."

- Limit controls to what's critical. A manager can maintain control over every little thing in his department or company. But in doing so, he'll also face the risk of overloading the system. Keep things simple; control only what's necessary.

- Avoid overcomplicated, involved plans. Nobody follows them anyway!

- Break down functions, if possible. Instead of forming large committees to do a lot of things, work with smaller, more controllable groups.

- Put the emphasis on doing a few things extremely well. That's infinitely more valuable than doing many things poorly.

"There is only one way to manage anything, and that is to keep it simple."
Theodore Leavitt

A Sucker for the Fad

No matter how silly the fad, many managers seem to hop right after it.

Too many business people are suckers for the fad. They go running after the new and improved machinery, the latest personality, the most recent buzzword, the most highly touted system.

They'll jump from management by objective to market segmentation to zero-based budgeting to positioning to long-range planning to PERT charts—and back again. Like little bunnies, they hop from one to another, hoping for the magic formula that's going to solve all their problems.

Mesmerized by a Machine

A simple example will show what I mean. Computers come on the scene. They become the "in" thing to get. Managers get them because they're now the thing to get. They have fancy lights and buttons and look pretty darn impressive. But one study estimated that over seventy percent of business computers are either unnecessary or are poorly used.

Sucker for a System

Here's another example. A government agency once had a systems analyst come in to help them with their work. Systems analysis was the latest thing. He treated everything as an abstraction, speaking in terms of mathematics, projections, flow charts. Everyone was wowed. Finally he left, his work completed. The dust settled. And soon everything was back to normal at the agency.

In the end his coming didn't have any effect at all, other than wasting some money and some time. Oh, he did accomplish one important thing: he allowed the agency to try out the latest fad!

Trying but Never Applying

One difficulty with fads is that people often don't consider whether the new machine or system is appropriate for their company. But sometimes the problem is not that the latest fad is worthless or even that it's unsuitable. It's that the latest fad seduces the business person into an inconsistent pattern. It makes him move away from the *last* idea before he's really given it a chance.

A new business idea comes out. "Okay," the boss says. "This is going to be the one that turns the company around." But he doesn't give it a chance. Because six months later an *even newer idea* is available.

During all this time the first idea has consistently been making some other organizations work very well.

Of course every organization has its idiosyncrasies, so you have to apply new ideas selectively, making sure you use only what fits your particular situation. The choice is yours.

But the real key is to be consistent. Don't jump from idea to idea. Don't make like a scared rabbit, dodging through the sagebrush. Settle on your management style, your work approach, and then stick with it and make it work. That's easy to say, of course. But it will take some effort to do.

Transfer through Concentration

Once you know an idea, person, technology has merit, how do you make it work in your organization? The secret is concentration.

Concentration is what makes any transfer work:

- If you want to transfer the power in one car battery to another battery, you must concentrate the power in the wires between the two batteries.

- If you want to transfer the heat from the sun to a paper, making it burn, you must concentrate the heat through a magnifying glass.

- If you want to transfer the life in a seed into a living plant, you must concentrate your efforts by leaving the seed in one place in the soil, putting the water in the same place each time, and so forth.

All too often potentially good managers fail because they fail to concentrate. They have the knowledge they need, but instead of concentrating it in one place, they waver around, hopping from one idea to another. In the end they're up to date but highly unproductive.

So what works? It's simple: **A concentration on proven people, principles, programs, or products is what produces the results.** Consistently.

Creative Procrastination

People always want things out of us. The creative procrastinator knows which to act on when.

Always put off until tomorrow those things that are irrelevant.

Some things are better off *not* done—at least not today:

Arnold's wife asked him to fix the dresser in the kids' bedroom. It was a sturdy old thing, but it needed a new paint job. And one leg was broken. Arnold had propped it up with a block of wood. When his wife asked him to fix it, Arnold had other priorities. "I'll do it later," he said. "Today I need to take care of the garden."

She asked him again. "I'll do it another time," he answered. "Today I have to do that project I brought home from work."

She asked again. "I'll do it tomorrow," he said. "For today, I need to make good on that promise to take the kids to the park for a picnic."

Arnold was a master at creative procrastination. He knew the dresser was just fine without the desired repairs. He had other things that were genuinely more important to do. It's been ten years since his wife first asked him to fix the dresser, and it's still not done.

"See, you just have to know my wife. She has this thing about having everything all nice and perfect. But it doesn't matter. Who cares whether the dresser is standing on a leg or a piece of wood? No one can see it under there. Besides, I'll get around to fixing it. Maybe tomorrow."

What are the negative effects of his procrastination? Only one: The dresser has to limp along unrepaired.

What are the positive effects? Many: He's been able to accomplish much. And his wife hasn't been too busy looking for *other* things for him to do.

Useless Meetings

John was the manager of public relations for his firm. He had an incredible number of meetings to attend. The firm felt that he could promote the firm best if he knew every little thing that was going on.

But the meetings weren't very useful. And he was invited to so many that he didn't have time to do any work. His eyes became tired from the strain; his brows were continually pressed together; and his wife complained that he was coming home too tired.

One day John asked himself, "What would happen if I stopped going to all these meetings?" As he thought about it, he realized the answer was "Nothing."

The next time he was invited to a meeting, he said, "I'll be by later."

Then: "I'll come to the meeting another time."

Then: "I'll come to the meeting tomorrow."

Suddenly John had plenty of time to get his work done. The meetings were no longer interfering. *And nothing bad happened!*

"Eventually they stopped asking me to come to the meetings," John says. "That was one of the best things I've accomplished since I've been with this company."

"We had these meetings, and the manager was totally incompetent in them. He'd fumble around with papers and waste our time. So John got fed up and stopped coming. Then another person stopped, and another. One day the manager came, and no one else was there. When he complained to the division head, the head put a stop to the meetings completely."

We've often heard of the importance of doing things. We constantly hear of how we should manage our time so we can get *everything* done.

But that's not the best way to boost production. Here's an even better approach. Decide what must be done, and decide what you can let go. Creatively procrastinate on whatever you can. If you have time later, do the less important things. Otherwise, forget them!

The Problem with Guilt

This idea works, of course, but most of us will have difficulty at first. We have a guilt complex inside our heads, a little voice that says, "If you don't do this, you're not a responsible person." Sometimes the voice is right—but just as often it's not. But we don't think about that. All we know is that little voice is inside badgering us. "You *should* be doing this. What will people think if you don't get it done?"

"Oh no! What have I done?"

When we fail to do what's asked of us, it's often difficult to get rid of guilt feelings.

Try a Test

We may feel guilty at first, but we don't have to stay that way. We can learn how wonderful the art of creative procrastination can be. Try a little test, and see how it feels. The next time someone asks you to do something that's really unimportant, tell them no. Or put them off.

When the world doesn't fall apart, you'll see that your guilty feelings were trying to mislead you. Now you'll have courage to say no to something bigger. Keep it up until it becomes a habit.

Note: Here's an idea to remember. The more separation there is between you and the person who wants you to do something, the easier it will be to avoid doing it. Having a client or a manager hanging over your shoulder is one of life's great miseries.

The Overworked Manager

A study was once done to see how well managers in a certain field were doing with their workload. The researchers asked two questions:

1. What are you supposed to do in your job? What are all the things that are expected of you?

2. How long does it take you to perform these functions?

The results of the study were astounding. The duties of the managers added up to 210 hours per week. And the week has only 168 hours in it—including sleeping and eating time!

No human being can do everything and anything that's asked of him. The effective manager will practice creative procrastination at every turn. He won't put off important things, of course. But he'll learn what must be done now and what can wait, and then he'll act accordingly.

The Key Question

In practicing the fine art of creative procrastination, you'll want to ask one key question: What would happen if I didn't do this thing?

Then carefully look at the answer. If you learn that nothing much will happen if you don't do it, don't do it! Keep putting it off until it becomes critical. And if it never becomes critical, you've found yourself some time to do something important.

What you don't do is often as important as what you do do.

Too Many Balls in the Air

Learning to Juggle

The juggler throws up his ball. It floats up, falls back down. He catches it and tosses it up again. He never misses.

Then he introduces a second ball. His task becomes a little more difficult. But he's able to handle it.

With more practice he's able to juggle three balls, then four, then five. But what if you give him five to start out with, when he's not even proficient with one? He'll drop them *all*. He won't even be able to handle one of them.

When we give people a job to do, it's like we're asking them to juggle. **The key to success is to give them enough balls to stretch their abilities, but not so many that they drop them all.** If we give them the right amount, we'll get some passable juggling, and their level of competence will gradually increase. As they become competent with one ball, they'll be able to learn how to handle two, then three.

Levels of Competence

To train people gradually takes money, time, and energy. But it's definitely the most effective approach. To give them five balls to juggle when they've never even handled one will cost even more in the long run.

Building levels of competence is like climbing a flight of stairs. You may want to take four steps at a time, but your legs aren't long enough. Instead, you need to take step one before you can move on to step two. Once you have sure footing on step two, you can move to step three.

Look at your company, and you may see the typical: the new worker is often overloaded, while the old worker is often underloaded.

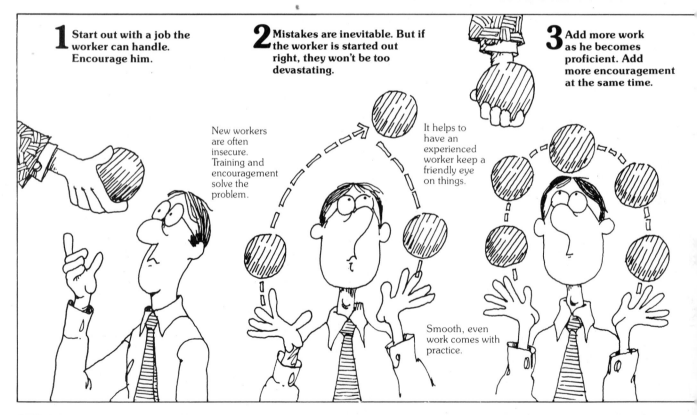

1 Start out with a job the worker can handle. Encourage him.

New workers are often insecure. Training and encouragement solve the problem.

2 Mistakes are inevitable. But if the worker is started out right, they won't be too devastating.

It helps to have an experienced worker keep a friendly eye on things.

Smooth, even work comes with practice.

3 Add more work as he becomes proficient. Add more encouragement at the same time.

What if you go too fast? You may skip a step, lose your footing, and fall back down to the bottom. Meanwhile, the other guy, who's proceeding more carefully, has arrived safely at the top.

The Incompetent File Clerk

A new file clerk joined an up-and-coming business. The boss had been minus a clerk for six weeks, and the load had piled up more and more every day. When he finally got his new clerk, he put him right to work. "Do this and do this, then this, this, and this. Then do this and this," he said.

The clerk's head began to spin. He was overloaded. He had too many balls to juggle. The boss was trying to push him up the stairs in one great leap.

The first day was a disaster. The next day was worse. At the end of the first week, the boss met with his assistants. "I'm afraid we've made

a bad mistake on this one," he told them. "This new fellow is totally incompetent."

Gradual Training

Of course the boss was wrong. What kind of results do you suppose he'd get if he had tried a different approach: "For the first couple of days I'd like you to become familiar with the filing system. Then we'll work on our company's system of circulating files."

Let people get good at juggling with one ball before you try to give them two or three.

It's vitally important that we don't overload our workers. But it's just as important that we give them more balls to juggle when they become proficient with the ones they have. If the manager doesn't give his best workers more balls to juggle, if the manager doesn't let them climb the next flight of stairs, they'll go elsewhere, finding someone who will give them what they want.

Note: Training is a critical but neglected area. It's too often poorly done or left out entirely. If a company wants to thrive, they should consider keeping track of what kind of training works and what doesn't and then make the necessary adjustments.

The Secret of Not Making Waves

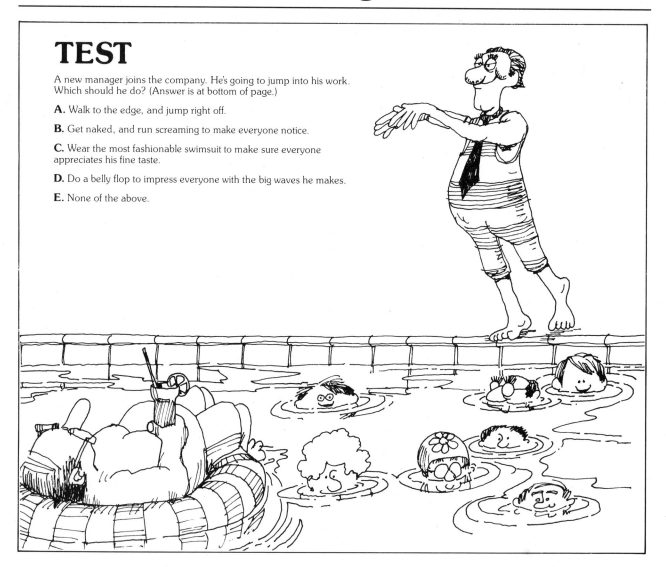

TEST

A new manager joins the company. He's going to jump into his work. Which should he do? (Answer is at bottom of page.)

A. Walk to the edge, and jump right off.

B. Get naked, and run screaming to make everyone notice.

C. Wear the most fashionable swimsuit to make sure everyone appreciates his fine taste.

D. Do a belly flop to impress everyone with the big waves he makes.

E. None of the above.

The New Manager

I know of a company that hired a red-hot new manager. He was supposed to turn things around, really make the business sizzle. The new man came in and took a quick look at how things stood. "What we need first of all is a new logo," he proclaimed.

It took him all of five minutes to come to that decision. It took him less than five seconds to make the pronouncement.

But that one little decision made a lot of waves. They started with the cost and time spent on

getting a new logo. Then everything had to be changed: forms, letterheads, brochures, business cards, company blazers, promotional items, the bronze symbol on the front of the building. Not to mention the incredible influence the old logo had on consumers' and clients' minds—which they lost with the new one.

The decision to change the logo was made on a whim. But the waves it caused washed throughout the company.

Then he moved on, and another new manager was hired. Yes, you guessed it. He put the

Answer: E (None of the above). He shouldn't do anything at all until he counts the cost.

76

stamp of his personality on the business, and the logo was changed again.

Before you ever jump in to act on anything, first count the cost. Every manager wants to put his mark on his business. But before you do, make sure it's worth the price you'll pay. A little act can have tremendous repercussions. It can stay with you till the day you die. That's okay, if the act and its repercussions are good. But if they are negative, you may regret that little act all your days.

It's Just a Small Stone

Making changes is like dropping a stone in the water. One little stone will make waves all across the pond. They ripple over, ripple back, ripple over again.

Every change you make will cause waves all across the pond, whether you think it will or not. Is it worth it?

In 1946 an earthquake occurred in the Aleutians. The underwater movement set off a series of waves in the ocean. Five hours and 2,300 miles later, those waves reached Hawaii. People and houses alike were swept out to sea by the force of those incredible seismic sea waves.

The people of Hawaii didn't feel the earthquake; they didn't even know about it. But they certainly experienced the effect of the waves.

Fighting the Dead

A good friend of mine recently married a widower. He had several children—and they weren't sure they wanted a new mom. My friend decided the only course was to be herself—to do the things she would normally do. That involved making some changes in her new household. I can't judge my friend, can't say what was right or wrong for her. But she did have a heavy task ahead of her. Everything she did was compared to the first wife. Everything she tried made waves. It wasn't worth it. Finally she gave up and just tried to go with the flow. "I'm tired of fighting the dead," she told me.

Changes in a Calm Pool

In a business in my area the founder recently retired. A new guy was brought in to head the company. He was in a tough spot. He moved into a calm pool—and tried to make changes. Everything he did was met with resistance.

Here are some key factors to keep in mind before you make any waves.

Size How big is the decision? How big will the waves be?

Speed How fast will the decision have an impact? The faster it hits, the fewer waves.

Expectation What do people expect? If they're prepared for some wave action, they can handle it better.

Time How long will it take for the change to be completed? How long can your workers hold their breath?

Distance How much will the decision affect a given set of workers? How close is the water to their nose?

Why? Because when you're sitting in the boat, you don't want someone to come along with his waves and rock it. You might fall out.

Constant Wave-Making

I once worked for a very wealthy businessman. He was so rich that his efforts in business were really just excuses to spend some of his money. He started in retail business. No—that wasn't what he wanted to do. He shifted into education. No, that didn't do it either. He moved his office to another city. No, that didn't fill his unmet need. He enlarged the business into a consulting firm. No. No. No.

Every move he made caused turmoil. None of his employees could stay with him for long. Not because he didn't want them, but because they couldn't take the constant shifting and wave-making. Even his wife finally left him.

Before You Make a Wave . . .

There's a real lesson here for all business people. Before you try to make any change

- *Count the cost.* Any change you make is going to make someone unhappy. Things take years to set up and get going. Change involves company employees physically, emotionally, and intellectually. What are the total costs of the change you're contemplating?

- *Make choices according to circumstances.* The more bureaucratic the company is, the less it will tolerate waves. In some firms, on the other hand, if you don't make waves, you're seen as not doing anything. Evaluate your own situation carefully to see how well your company environment can handle the changes you have in mind.

- *Compare values.* Is what you're getting of as much value as what you're giving up? Don't deny a change that's needed—but do be sure you know what you're getting into.

- *Ask the question, "Is it worth it?"* If the answer is *no*, then forget your idea. Sometimes the waves are so bad that the change just isn't worth it even if change is needed. But if the answer to your question is *yes*, then *act*. Don't mess around. Oscillating between your courses of action will cost you and your organization even more.

A stupid choice by one person can have devastating results.

"Help!"

"He's ruined what I've been working on for a year!"

"Kill that man!"

"Oh, no!"

"Arggh!"

"Show off!"

Trivia Overload

Trivia can gum up the works, even to the point that nothing important can move.

Dribble and trivia drown out critical thinking and acting. It takes constant reaffirmation of what the business is about to stay above it all.

The Copy Machine Caper

It started with Robert's new assignment to get the copy center running smoothly.

His first move was to issue a memo to every single soul in the office complex. The memo instructed us that free use of any copy machine was a definite no-no. But up until that time everyone understood an unwritten rule. It was that anyone who worked there could make a few copies for themselves. But with the memo, that ended.

Then a war started between Robert and the personal copy thief. The first skirmish began with unaccounted-for copies showing up on the copy center records.

Robert retaliated with a huge sign on the copy center door—absolutely, positively forbidding personal use. But with the next accounting it was obvious the personal copy maker had struck again.

Robert immediately called a meeting (mandatory attendance, of course) and threw down the ultimatum. He stated flatly, "Someone is stealing from our company, and if they don't stop, they will receive harsh disciplinary action." But Robert had to catch them first.

The petty pilferage continued, and Robert's efforts had no effect. He was obsessed with discovering who it was and putting the culprit to some well-deserved gruesome end.

For days Robert stayed at work past closing hours. On one of the late sessions he heard the criminal making his illegal copies behind the closed door.

Robert burst in yelling like a cop catching bank robbers. His yelling quickly lowered into incoherent mumbles. He turned his back, lowered his head, and shuffled back out of the center, carefully closing the door behind him very quietly.

The copy culprit was Michael—the company president.

A short time later Wilma, from personnel, came by and showed me something. It was the total cost for the copy machine caper. What the whole escapade cost the company, she said, was almost $4,000. I couldn't believe her.

She then went over each cost line by line. She added up people's time reading memos, attending meetings, and gossiping about the whole affair. Wilma also added all the time and materials Robert used up.

After she went over it all, discussing in detail each item, I'm convinced it was a conservative estimate.

Oh, by the way, I figure our conversation about the caper cost about $62.

Trivialize: The well-practiced art of turning a little into a lot; over-managing mole hills into bureaucratic mountains; turning the location of where the office picnic will be into a major policy decision.

Impatience Can Kill

We live in an impatient society. Everything's got to happen NOW! We want:

Want something and want it now? Okeydokey. Just add water and stir, and there it is!

An Impatient Society

This impatience permeates our society. We want everything now, and if we can't have it now, we want it sooner. We typically have to stand in lines to get served in stores; we have to wait in restaurants. But instead of relaxing we complain: "Why do we have to stand in line?" "All we ever do is hurry up and wait!" "If I have to stand in line one more time, I think I'll scream!"

Television networks will give a new show a couple of weeks to build an audience, and if it fails, they pull it—sometimes before a lot of viewers even know it exists. I've had food literally thrown at me by waitresses. Somehow they felt that speed was more important than courtesy.

Impatience can kill. Some things take time to develop. In fact, the very thing you want most probably takes time—and impatience will take it away from you.

See if this mentality seems familiar:

"You have a new idea? Great! What, you haven't seen any benefit yet? Well, better kill it and try something else."

"We tried a new process, but it didn't prove itself fast enough. We decided to forget it."

"That new person hasn't learned to perform yet. Fire him!"

Some things, some great things, take time:

- A baby
- A tree
- Reaching the Super Bowl
- A new idea
- A productive company

"Those who cannot wait never win."

Buddha

Turning Employees into Lead—or Gold?

The ancient wizard enters his dark and musty dungeon and begins to stir his pot. Strange odors waft through the room. A spider creeps down his elaborate web in the corner to watch more closely. "Wing of bat, hair of toad," the wizard mumbles. "Poison mushroom, witch's wart, vampire blood. Mix together," he mutters to himself as he puts in more and more ingredients. The room fills with smoke.

Then he drops in a piece of lead. "Now!" he shouts. The floor shakes. The cauldron shifts over the fire. Bottles clink against one another on the shelves that line the room. Pouches of strange herbs swing from the roof beams. Then the wizard raises his hand, and the room becomes still. He leans way over and peers into the cauldron. Deep in the bottom, down through murky water, he sees a glint of gold. An eerie look comes into his eyes, and he smiles as he strokes his long gray beard.

Many centuries have passed, but the ancient art of alchemy remains in force.

The Reversal in an Ancient Art

Wizards of olden times ever sought to perfect their craft, trying to turn lead into gold, but modern wizards are more successful. The ancient art of alchemy has been replaced by the modern art of ineptitude—and its practitioners are infinitely successful at turning gold into lead. It's a real skill, and many people have learned it to perfection.

They see a woman and think *secretary*. After all, if a person is a woman, she must be able to type and take phone calls, but she probably isn't trained to do much else. With this preconception, they may take a person of pure gold, someone who has all kinds of skills, and permanently pigeonhole her as a secretary. Now, there's nothing wrong with secretaries; their skills are invaluable to every company. But—surprise!—many women make better

Shown here are the latest recipients of the MBA (Masters of Business Alchemy) degree. The professor is shown on the left.

managers than secretaries. (And—double surprise!—many men make superb secretaries.)

In an electronics firm some of the technicians have some great ideas for moving ever onward and upward. But management doesn't see it, and they won't provide support. Result: the technicians finally quit and start their own company. The first company had gold on its hands. But with a great deal of care they were able to turn the gold into lead.

Forcing people into the wrong position can only cause frustration and failure—in both you and them. Not allowing people to grow and expand can result only in pain and loss.

Gold is turned into lead when

- Management forces skilled people into slots where they don't fit.

- Management won't take the effort or the time or the money to make the most of their people.

A Golden Combination

Not too long ago there was a kid in my area who really loved to play football. All through high school he played—but he was a pass receiver on a rushing team. He never got the chance to show what he could do.

As a result, when he went to junior college, he was a walk-on on the team. No one knew who he was. And no one seemed to care. It got more and more discouraging until finally the kid decided to quit. He stopped going to practice, and nobody even noticed. Except the quarterback.

"Hey, you can't quit," the quarterback told him. "You have a lot of talent hidden in you."

The quarterback talked him into coming back. "Let's both make All-American."

Every night they'd put in extra practice. But it didn't seem to do much good. The coach wouldn't see the gold in either of them. He wouldn't let the quarterback call his own plays, and he wouldn't let the receiver play.

Six games went by, and the team lost every one of them. The seventh game came. The team was behind 6-0, and only nineteen seconds were left. The team got the ball at the far end of the field—and the coach just shook his head. "Just go out there, and do what you want," he shouted at the quarterback. "There's no way you guys can move the ball. You've been unable to the whole game."

"Okay," said the quarterback. "But let my friend play."

In the nineteen seconds that were remaining, the quarterback and the receiver finally had a chance to show their gold. The quarterback was calling his own plays. And the receiver was out on the field. In just nineteen seconds they moved the entire length of the field and made a touchdown. And an extra point.

Then the coach saw the possibilities. He let them go into the next game—and they won. They won every game the rest of the season. They won the conference the next year. And both players became All-American.

The gold was always there.

Note: Some things we need to test out before we know what they're made of. We can't tell the composition of some metals, for instance, until we put them through a testing process. The same is true of many people.

What If Someone Drops the Bucket?

Cold Creek, 10:00 A.M.

Cold Creek, 4:00 P.M.

"Where's my bucket?"

We often have to rely on a critical person at a critical time. But if they fail, we find ourselves in deep trouble.

The Cold Creek Bucket Brigade

The town of Cold Creek in Oregon Territory was thriving. It had three saloons, a hotel, a general store, and various other signs of civilization. Cold Creek even had its own sheriff, though, admittedly, it was only a part-time job. Mail was brought in every Monday. And on Friday and Saturday nights, every week, the people in the area gathered at the Cold Bucket for a little dancin' and romancin'.

There was only one thing Cold Creek lacked: a fire department. There wasn't much use for one, really. In the town's eighteen years of existence, it had experienced only one serious fire, and that was limited to the parson's woodpile, which was located behind the cemetery. The parson lost nearly all his wood—but the townspeople pitched in and helped him renew the pile.

Who needs a fire department, anyway, when you have a skilled bucket brigade? That's what Cold Creek's city fathers thought, and they were probably right. The critical word there, of course, was *skilled*.

Once a month, the Cold Creek Bucket Brigade had a fire drill. At one moment the members of

the brigade would be going about their own business of minding the store or serving the bar; the next moment they'd be out responding to the clanging of the bell, buckets in hand.

But one day the bell clanged, and it wasn't just a drill. The blacksmith's shop was on fire! The members of the brigade quickly took their places, buckets in hand. All except Oscar Jeppson, that is. Old Oscar couldn't find his bucket.

The Missing Bucket

The members of the brigade worked frantically, doing their best. They nearly had the fire contained, but they were one bucket short. Their rhythm was off; their resources were just a touch diminished by Oscar's absence. They dipped and hauled and handed and sweated—then watched with wide eyes, horrified, as the fire jumped from the blacksmith shop to the livery stable . . .

Before the afternoon was over, the entire town was gone. Oscar Jeppson was still looking for his bucket.

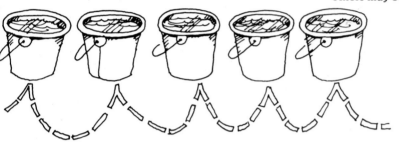

When one element is out of whack, the efforts of all the others may be wasted.

If just one key function fails, it can ruin your whole effort. The more complex your organization, the more critical each part becomes.

In a well-constructed organization, every element is critical. **If a key element fails to perform, it must be removed or the entire organization will suffer.**

The whole town may burn down if every member of the brigade isn't present.

The person who isn't performing well may have great aptitude as a brain surgeon, a wandering minstrel, or a jelly bean polisher. But if he isn't doing his job on the bucket brigade, get him out!

As you look at your organizational problems, you'll find that they can't all be laid at the feet of poor Oscar Jeppson. The difficulties run deeper than that. If Oscar was so critical, why wasn't there a backup for him?

Always Have a Backup

- When NASA sends a satellite into space, they always have a backup for each primary function. Then if the main system fails, the controllers turn to the backup.

- When a basketball team is going down to the wire, with one final chance to win the game, they rely on a key player to make the critical shot. But if they're smart, they also have a backup, a player standing by to try again if the key player fails.

- When a doctor schedules a critical surgery, he doesn't plan to do it alone. The risks are too great. He has a second doctor assisting him, a reliable surgeon who can serve as a backup if things go awry.

Should our organizations do any less? Can we assume that the key person in the organizational structure will never let us down? If we do, we may discover all too late that our personal Cold Creek is smoldering in ruins.

"At last! There's my bucket!"

A Powerful Method for Getting Cooperation

Too often business finds itself in the middle of a great civil war. Every part of the U.S. economy breaks off into a separate army, fighting all the others. It's government versus labor versus management versus consumer versus government versus management and so on and on. It's front office versus back shop versus supplier versus shipper.

We're all dependent on each other. Why do we insist on warring against each other?

The usual way things get done is for the people on top of the pile to make a decision. The troops are then handed their marching orders and are expected to march.

Root binding takes a lot of time and effort to achieve. But once it's done, you'll be able to move faster than ever before, and your chances of success will increase significantly.

The more people participate and agree on a decision, the more involved they'll be in carrying it out.

Root Binding

The Japanese put an idea to work, to good effect. They call their approach *nemawashi*— root binding. The idea is to treat people as carefully as one would treat a plant. When you want to transplant a tree, you don't just pull it up and replant it. You carefully dig around the roots, making sure you don't sever any. Once the tree's been taken from the ground, you wrap all the roots together before you start to move it. By taking such precautions, you'll have a live tree in the end, rather than a dead one.

The techniques for moving a tree and moving people are much the same.

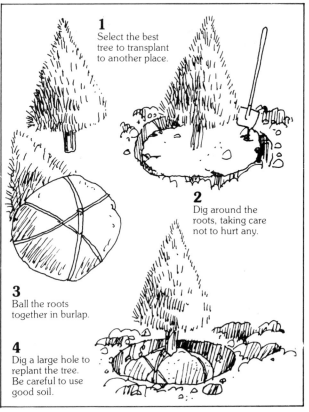

1 Select the best tree to transplant to another place.

2 Dig around the roots, taking care not to hurt any.

3 Ball the roots together in burlap.

4 Dig a large hole to replant the tree. Be careful to use good soil.

The same approach works with people. Before the Japanese leaders make an important decision, they get the input of the people. They find out what everyone wants. Only when they've reached a consensus of opinion will they move ahead.

Root binding is a time-consuming process. It drives western leaders bonkers. But it *works*. If you don't take the time at first, you'll just waste even more time in replanting.

"M.A.S.H." Binding

Probably everyone has at one time or another watched the popular TV show "M.A.S.H." While other shows were coming and going around it, "M.A.S.H." continued to draw large audiences. What was the secret to its success?

One answer is that they used the root-binding approach. The show was structured so that everyone on the cast had a chance to be involved, to make a contribution beyond their acting assignment. During the filming season, the actors and writers and producers would periodically meet to discuss the script, to refine and perfect it. At one time or another, different members of the cast had the opportunity to try directing a show.

The result of all their effort—and the broad involvement of many members of the "M.A.S.H." staff—was a TV show that proved to be a personal investment for all involved. Not to mention the good entertainment for everyone else.

Root binding isn't easy. It's usually slower than any other approach. But it does have one great thing going for it. It calls a truce to the civil war. It gets people working together again, instead of at odds with each other.

Building an effective team can be long, hard work. But the rewards consistently prove its value.

The 80/20 Rule

In the late 1800s, Italian economist Vilfredo Pareto noticed that 20 percent of his countrymen controlled 80 percent of the wealth and power in Italy.

The 80/20 Rule

It was a simple enough discovery. But from that has come the 80/20 rule. In a lot of things in life, 80 percent of the results tend to be produced by 20 percent of the activity.

- **80** percent of the country's employee problems are caused by **20** percent of the employees.

Most of the trouble is caused by 20 percent of the work force.

- **80** percent of the energy in a neutron bomb is released in high-speed neutrons, and **20** percent in heat and blast.

- **80** percent of a company's phone use usually comes from **20** percent of the employees.

- **80** percent of all university research grants are obtained by **20** percent of the professors.

- **80** percent of your file use is from only **20** percent of your files.

We regularly use very few of our files.

- **80** percent of the choices made from a restaurant's menu are made from **20** percent of the items.

- **80** percent of the energy in an automobile engine is wasted; **20** percent runs the car.

- **80** percent of the energy fed into a light bulb is given off in heat; **20** percent is given off in light.

Most electricity for lights goes up in heat.

- **80** percent of your sales comes from **20** percent of your customers.

A few customers always seem to be the ones you do the most business with, and you make the most money from still fewer.

- **80** percent of the goods of the world are controlled by **20** percent of the people.

- **80** percent of a company's complaints come from only **20** percent of the customers.

- **80** percent of downtime in a factory is caused by **20** percent of the machines.

Learn Concentration

The 80/20 rule teaches a simple, but important, lesson: **Concentrate on the 20 percent.** Put value in where you'll get value out. If 80 percent of the results come from 20 percent of the effort, capitalize on that positive 20 percent. Shift your emphasis so that you're spending less time with the negative 80 percent. That doesn't apply to just time use, either. The rule applies to people, products, processes, inventory, materials, machines—everything.

Deemphasize the 80

One management investment group specializes in rescuing failing companies. Through their experience they've learned that such companies almost always have one thing in common: the company is spending 80 percent of its time and money and energy to get 20 percent of its results. That means, to reverse it, that the other 80 percent of the results are coming from only 20 percent of the effort.

Emphasize the 20

The investment group does a simple thing: they shift the company's emphasis. They start using the strengths of the positive 20 percent and lop off a lot of the deadwood.

It's a lesson all of us have to learn if we hope to do more than survive—if we hope to thrive.

If you want to increase productivity, you need to spend more time and resources on your productive 20 percent. This takes constant effort. The natural tendency is to rest on the comfortable 80.

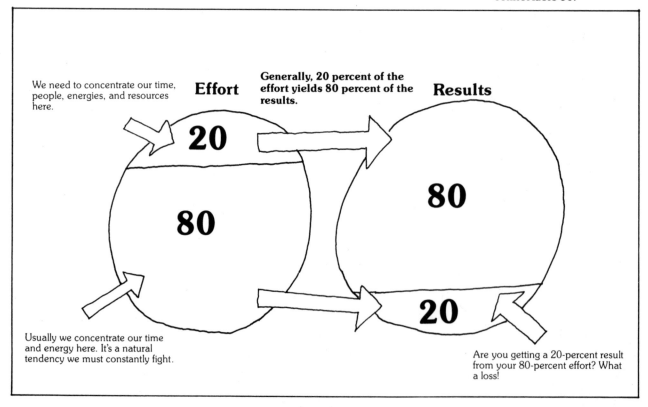

We need to concentrate our time, people, energies, and resources here.

Effort

Generally, 20 percent of the effort yields 80 percent of the results.

Results

Usually we concentrate our time and energy here. It's a natural tendency we must constantly fight.

Are you getting a 20-percent result from your 80-percent effort? What a loss!

The 80/20 rule describes a general tendency. But all too often the relationship is more on a ratio of 90/10.

The Destructive Promotion

I knew a glassworker who was one of the best in his field. He took pride in his craft; he took pride in constantly improving. Whenever he completed an important job, he'd drive his family past the building and show them the work he'd done on it.

But every silver lining has a cloud. This glassworker did such outstanding work that his company promoted him and made him a foreman. With the promotion his function changed drastically. Instead of working with glass, which he was so proficient at, he was now assigned to work with people. His job involved checking up on the work of others, keeping contractors happy in the process.

All he saw every day was problems. Instead of having a feeling of accomplishment in finishing a job, he was able only to heave a sigh of relief that another problem was over. When he'd drive his family past buildings he'd been involved with, he couldn't show them his good work. All he could see was another's mistakes.

Moving Up to Failure

I know an office manager who had a similar problem. She was super at her job—well-organized, efficient, good at motivating others and delegating work. The company officials had their eye on this woman for quite a while, and they were rather impressed with her ability. One day they came to her with a nice surprise: a big raise and a promotion to being an officer in the company.

There was only one catch: her job changed at the same time. Now instead of running the office she spent her days interviewing people. From eight in the morning to five at night she'd interview others. At the end of each day she'd look back on what she'd accomplished—and she felt that she hadn't accomplished anything. "All I do all day every day is sit on my can and *talk* to people," she complained.

"Congratulations, you've done an excellent job as a fish. Now we're going to move you up to being a bird!"

Authority tends to assign jobs to those least able to do them.
Cornvelle's Law

One week was all it took to make her climb the walls. She went back to her bosses and asked for a *demotion*. The money and status just weren't worth the hassle that came with them.

Promotions aren't always a step up. Often they're a whole flight of steps down—and out.

The Peter principle says that people rise to the level of incompetence. That rise is usually a promotion given by a person saying the words, "They're doing such a good job let's move them up." People are promoted to the point where their personalities and skills no longer fit their work. They can't be competent.

Promotion is a dangerous word. Usually we feel that if we don't move up the ladder, we're failures. But that's not necessarily the case; it's certainly not when the position we're in *now* is just right for us. If we're in the **right place at the right time doing the right thing,** it's too bad when someone comes along with the misguided bright idea of moving us.

In Love with Numbers

I know a person who worked as a statistician. He loved to manipulate figures. Given any kind of problem that dealt with figures, he'd work it out just for the fun of it.

This person had a good job. It let him do what he did best. He liked working by himself, doing his job with statistics, having control of his own environment.

But then the management struck. They liked his work, so they "promoted" him. They put him in charge of a shop with twenty people in it. They gave him a budget. All day long my friend hassled with people, trying to motivate them, trying to get them to meet their deadlines. At least once an hour someone was in his office complaining.

It wasn't long before he got sick. He couldn't function in his new job. Finally he went to another company, where they let him do what he did best.

Promoted Right

One woman was hired to be a secretary. She was qualified on paper, but she wasn't really suited for the job. Everyday she'd dread going to work. She tried hard but couldn't make things go smoothly. Just because she was a woman didn't mean she was automatically a good secretary.

Then the management decided they needed a troubleshooter to work with people problems in the company. They noticed that this woman had a good ability to talk with others, and they offered the new job to her.

All day long she'd hear people talk out their problems to her. She dealt with difficult staff problems, with customer complaints—and she loved it! Staff morale improved. Customer relations improved. And the ex-secretary came to work with a new spring in her step.

Find a Good Fit

When you're working with others, recognize that each person has different abilities. Each has different personality traits. And different goals and desires. Find what fits your people— and then let them do what they do well.

Don't promote someone just to promote them. Don't promote a good worker just because he's doing well where he is. If someone is doing an outstanding job, good rewards can come in the form of increased benefits or salary. But think twice before you promote.

When you do decide to promote one of your workers, promote him to a position where he can use his strengths, not his weaknesses. Promote him to a place where he'll *fit*.

Three Ideas for Dealing with the Double Bind

The double bind pushes you in two directions at once.

The Deadly Double Bind

Virtually every organization I know is locked in some kind of a double bind. It has different characteristics for different companies, but it holds them tight in every case. Here are some of the ways the double bind can show up:

- The more satisfied the customers are, the bigger the company will grow. But the bigger the company grows, the wider the gap between management and customers becomes. And the customers become less and less satisfied.

- The more that similar companies could work together, the more they could increase their exports, like foreign competition does. But the more they work together, the quicker the antitrust people jump on them to shut them down.

- The way to stay alive in agriculture is to produce more. But the more you produce, the lower prices go—and the more precarious your situation becomes.

- Stockholders demand short-term profits, but that decreases long-term investment, which cuts down on tomorrow's profits.

- Employees want to quit at five o'clock like everyone else—but that's the best time for your customer to come into the store.

- Your company's survival depends on innovation, but innovation is exactly what the company's structure is designed to discourage.

- Consumers want lower prices, but all your costs are going up.

- You're working for a family-owned company and want to move up—but nephew Harold just started to work. Yet you're not willing to quit.

- You're expected to eat crackers while whistling Bach.

Here is an actual photograph of what the Deadly Double Bind looks like!

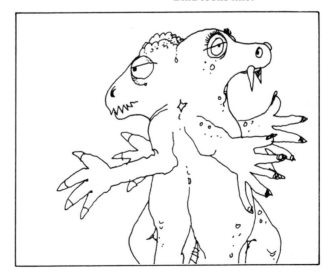

Note: Even cockeyed optimists have been known to be put to bed by a double bind.

A No-Win Situation

I think you can identify with some of the previous situations. They fit all of us. And they give all of us fits, because it is hard to get into a double bind and win. When you're caught between opposites, you'll invariably lose in one direction as you win in the other. While you please one side, the other thinks you're the biggest failure that ever walked the face of the earth.

Okay, so you can't win. What do you do? Try one of these:

1 Accept the Frustration.

There is some emotional relief in accepting something that can't be changed.

Take the frustration you feel, and try to vent it constructively. That excludes the most common approach: go out and invite an ulcer to join you. Some people take up a hobby. Some play racquetball. Some jog. The most frustrating thing about this is that it's often the only action available.

2 Transfer the Bind.

If you pass the double bind to someone else, you won't have to worry about it any more.

Give it away to someone else. One manager transferred his double bind problem to his stockholders. He sent them a letter: "You say you want short-term profits. You want a nice dividend every year. Fine. But if we do that, we'll be giving you the money we need to invest back into the company to keep it strong and alive for many years to come. We'll be stealing from Peter (tomorrow's investment) to pay Paul (your dividend). So which will it be? You own the company: do you want some money now, or do you want a strong investment for many years to come?"

3 Force a Choice.

By making a hard choice, you cut through the double bind, changing your circumstances.

This is the hardest approach of all, and sometimes it's impossible. But it may be worth a try.

Ryan disliked his in-laws so much that he'd never visit them. His wife, Jenny, struggled with the double bind for years—she wanted to see her folks, but she also wanted her husband to be with her. Finally, she made a choice: she took the kids and went alone. After she'd gone alone a few times, Ryan decided he didn't like to stay at home—and he started to go with her.

An electronics firm in San Diego, California, was caught in a double bind: they wanted to keep their prices competitive, but they also had to pay union wages. They cut through the bind by making a critical choice—they moved across the border to Mexico, where the labor was cheaper.

Being caught in a double bind is one of the least productive states a person can get stuck in.

Too Many Hands Make Hard Work

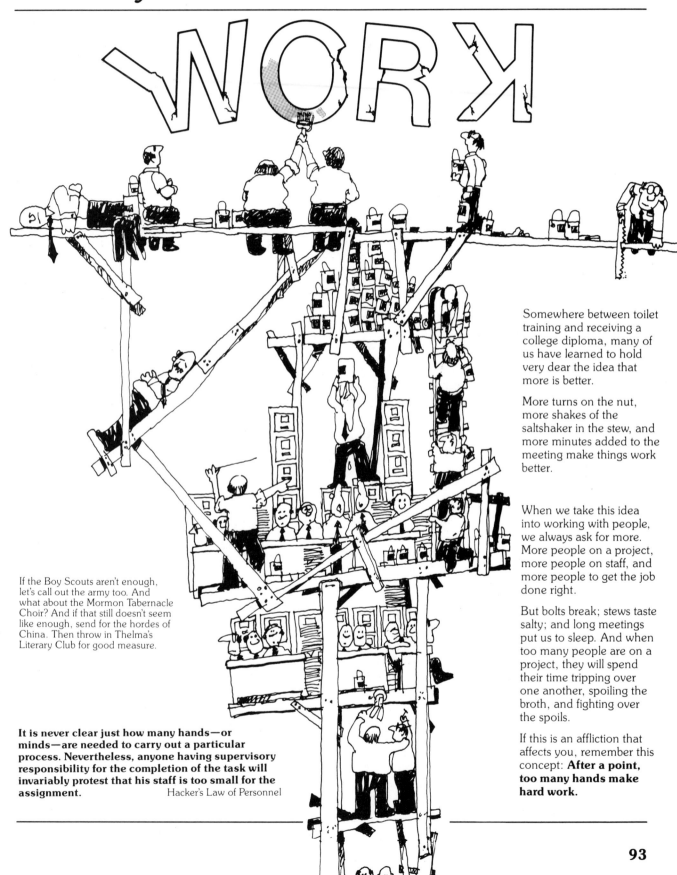

Somewhere between toilet training and receiving a college diploma, many of us have learned to hold very dear the idea that more is better.

More turns on the nut, more shakes of the saltshaker in the stew, and more minutes added to the meeting make things work better.

When we take this idea into working with people, we always ask for more. More people on a project, more people on staff, and more people to get the job done right.

But bolts break; stews taste salty; and long meetings put us to sleep. And when too many people are on a project, they will spend their time tripping over one another, spoiling the broth, and fighting over the spoils.

If this is an affliction that affects you, remember this concept: **After a point, too many hands make hard work.**

If the Boy Scouts aren't enough, let's call out the army too. And what about the Mormon Tabernacle Choir? And if that still doesn't seem like enough, send for the hordes of China. Then throw in Thelma's Literary Club for good measure.

It is never clear just how many hands—or minds—are needed to carry out a particular process. Nevertheless, anyone having supervisory responsibility for the completion of the task will invariably protest that his staff is too small for the assignment. Hacker's Law of Personnel

Following the Leader into Trouble

The Bond Fiasco

When the city's largest bank decided to invest in bonds in a foreign country, the other banks sat up and took notice. The reasoning was that they'd be able to invest at a high rate of interest. Then they could borrow new money at a low rate and lend it out at a higher rate. They'd make money both coming and going.

"If it's good enough for the big bank, then it's good enough for me," the smaller banks said. And they invested their money too.

It seemed like an investment made in heaven. The only problem was that the project the bonds were funding collapsed, and the foreign country defaulted on its bond debt. Losing all that money was difficult for the large bank, but it was devastating for the smaller ones. They wondered why they'd trusted the judgment of the large bank.

If you insist on following the leader, at least keep your eyes on where you're going. Too often companies look to another company for guidance—but often the company that's doing the guiding doesn't know anything either.

It's a case of the blind leading the blind. If you're going to follow a blind man, at least make sure you take your own cane along.

Keeping Up with the Joneses

A good name for the problem is "metooism." The Joneses buy a new car, and the neighbors say "Me too!" The Joneses turn their garage into a party room, and the neighbors say, "Me too!"

Metooism makes the assumption that the other guy knows where he's going. And that the place he's going is good for everyone else. Those assumptions can be deadly.

The Computer Disaster

A large company was invited to tie into a new computer system in a neighboring state. The system salesman said it was the best thing going. "We can serve the needs of any kind of company," he said. The initial investment was large. "But it will be worth it," the salesman said.

Smaller companies were watching. "Maybe that would be good for us, too," they said. And they also tied into the system.

Soon everyone involved found that the computer system was inadequate for their needs. The system was down a lot. And when it was going, it was often overloaded by the companies that had bought its services.

In the end, everyone, the large company included, backed out. They bought their own, smaller systems. At another big cost.

"If only we hadn't played follow-the-leader!" the small companies moaned.

NOTE: Making a unique and important contribution is often better than following a leader down his path, especially if he has been on that path a long time.

The Smart Construction Company

A construction firm in a major city was concerned about costs. "What can we do to cut the basic costs of our operation?" the leaders asked each other.

They talked it over and finally decided to make a drastic, but brilliant, move. They would get rid of most of their employees, thereby eliminating hassles, extra Social Security payments, extra taxes, and other such problems. But they wouldn't leave the employees high and dry. They'd use them as subcontractors on all their jobs.

It seemed to be a perfect move. They could continue to work on all the jobs they had before, maintaining their leadership position in the city, and at the same time cut their costs a great deal.

The smaller companies in the area saw what their larger competitor had done, and it seemed to make sense. They decided to follow suit. Only one held back. "Let's see if this really works," they said.

Before long the city was filled with the skeletons of formerly large construction companies—and an overabundance of independent contractors. And before long the firm that had started it all found that its former employees were bidding against the larger construction firm.

Only one company had the clout to consistently get the bids on new projects. It was the company that had refused to follow the group. The one who wouldn't follow the leader quickly grew and became the most profitable company in the business. The others, because they were unable to handle the larger, more profitable jobs, dwindled and some failed totally.

Often it doesn't pay to follow a leader. He may take you right into trouble.

It's easy to follow the pack. But first we should find out where we're going!

"Remember, I'm next!"

If It Isn't Broken, Don't Fix It

"Where in the hell are the chicks? It's been twenty-three days, and I've helped you continually!"

Sometimes the helper gets more in the way than he helps!

Carl was going at fifty miles per hour on his motorcycle. It was running pretty well, but Carl was a perfectionist, and he thought he could improve things. If the carburetor was adjusted just a little . . . He leaned over and began to fiddle with it, keeping one hand on the handle bars.

It wasn't too surprising when Carl crashed his motorcycle on the side of the road.

Tinkering can be dangerous. Oftentimes things will be going well in a company, but the management just can't resist doing a little tinkering. They never leave well enough alone. They make just a little change here, a little adjustment there. But sometimes just one more little addition or change can kill the whole thing.

"If it ain't broke, don't fix it." Bert Lance

Southern Fried Chicken

Billy Joe ran a restaurant that specialized in southern foods. The food was outstanding, and the clientele was loyal. Profits were very respectable. But Billy Joe was a fiddler; he couldn't keep his hands off success:

"Maybe we should change the menu here," he said.

"Maybe we should change the prices on these items," he said.

"Maybe we should adjust our hours."

"Maybe we could get by with three fewer waitresses."

Billy Joe fiddled too much and too long, and eventually he ended up without a business at all. All the years of effort, all the money expended—down the drain. It's really too bad—he had the best fried chicken anywhere!

Before a person messes with something that's already working, he or she should ask one vital question: "Am I tinkering, or am I fixing?" If the answer is "tinkering," leave it alone. Every business is subject to the law of diminishing returns; every person reaches the point where the value gained isn't worth the added effort. In fact, the returns can diminish to the point where the effort expended will bring only *negative* returns!

Tinkering or Fixing?

In my career, I've noticed that most managing is overmanaging. The manager does too much too often. If only we could learn that many things are better off left alone!

If you mess with a thing long enough, it'll break.
Schmidt's Law

Climbing Out of the Rut

It's true that tinkering with something that's already working can be dangerous, but it's also dangerous not to keep an eye out for needed changes.

When we're digging a ditch (rut), it's hard to see anything but dirt. If we look too closely at our work for too long a period of time, we get so we can't see very far away. We get so we can't see what's coming at us.

There's only one reliable way to see the consequences of what we're doing: periodically climb up out of the ditch to get a higher view.

Doug "Digger" Benton could outdig any other digger.

Doug "Digger" Benton was the top man in the whole Water District. He could start a ditch and be farther down the path faster than any other ditchdigger. Digger had three grades of shovels to use in the different kinds of soil he encountered, and he kept each one of them razor-sharp. His fellow workers in the Water District liked to joke about his dedication: "Digger wouldn't even know the sun had gone down if we didn't tell him." He was just too busy doing a good job.

When visitors to the ditch came by, the foreman always took them to Digger's section. He took real pride in his craftsmanship, and he'd gladly show them the technique in getting straight sides.

One day when Digger was busy doing his job, the company officials decided to buy a ditch-digging machine. "We have men like Digger who do great work," they said. "But they just can't compete with today's technology."

Digger didn't even see the ditchdigger coming at him. He was too busy digging.

Matt "Big Spoon" Washington could finish a ditch in just hours.

Matt "Big Spoon" Washington was the best heavy-equipment operator in the whole Water District. He could start and finish a ditch in a matter of hours, leaving his co-workers back in the dust. Matt was able to dig in impossible corners. He had pinstripes on his Caterpillar, with a CB inside, and he could ride it up mounds that were steeper than steep and then come back down again. In fact, "Big Spoon" was so good at his work that he often had a gallery of onlookers watching him dig.

Matt's fellow workers liked to joke about how diligent he was: "Matt would rather dig than eat," they said. "And you ought to see the incredibly wonderful job he does."

Matt was so busy digging that he didn't notice when the Water District closed down their ditch operations. "Sprinklers are the wave of the future. They're making ditches obsolete," they said.

Suzy "Copper Pipe" Ortega made ditches obsolete.

The Water District brought in Suzy "Copper Pipe" Ortega to help them convert to sprinklers. She immediately immersed herself in her work . . .

Established technology tends to persist in spite of new technology.

Full Lions Don't Hunt

"There are times when you don't need to worry, and this is one of them."

The Tale of Bruce and Rodney

An ancient tale is told of the fierce lion and the luckless antelopes he hunted. The lion ranged far and wide, stalking his prey, until he finally fell upon one of the antelopes, ripping into it and pulling it down.

The antelopes scattered in fear. The lion didn't pay attention. He bit with powerful jaws into the bloody meat of the antelope, gorging himself on the flesh.

One of the antelopes, named Bruce, watched for a moment, then started to walk over to the lion. His younger friend Rodney shouted out in alarm. "Don't go over there! Look, the lion has already killed Roger. Do you want to get killed too?"

By now Bruce was standing right by the lion and started to graze contentedly, not concerned in the least. "Don't get all lathered up, my boy," Bruce said. "As you get older, you'll learn what I know: full lions don't hunt!"

What's true with lions and antelopes is also true with all kinds of human organizations. **Dissatisfaction stirs effort. Satisfaction leads to inactivity.**

When a company is lean and mean, it will expend a great deal of energy trying to get satisfaction.

But when it gets fat and self-satisfied, it starts taking things easy. No problems and no competition; no hunger and no effort.

A Couple of Fat and Self-satisfied Companies

A good example is Xerox Corporation. They had a firm grip on the copier market. But they had little competition. They were a full lion. The Japanese sneaked up on them and started to graze. At one point Xerox shares sold at a price-to-earnings ratio of eighty-eight. By late 1981 the ratio had fallen as low as six. Their share of the U.S. market used to be ninety-six percent. By late 1981 it had fallen to forty-six percent.

Their product was as valuable as ever. But they'd gotten so fat they didn't even notice the competition coming in on them—or they didn't believe it could happen.

Chrysler Corporation gives us another good example. During the 1960s the company grew very comfortable with their performance, moving from a market share of ten percent to eighteen percent. They were so happy with their growth, in fact, that they sat complacent through most of the 1970s and didn't bother to adjust with the times. The result? In 1980 the company had to reorganize completely, with the help of a $1.2 billion loan guaranteed by the government.

The Kids against the Seasoned Pros

Compare that to the new kid on the block, the organization that doesn't have the luxury of sitting on its laurels.

In the 1980 Winter Olympics, people throughout the United States thrilled as the U.S. hockey team made its way through the eliminations. Virtually every team it met was favored against it—and the U.S. team still won.

Then the team came up against the tough Russian team. There was no chance, the experts said. The U.S. team ("Why, they're just kids!") had been lucky, but the trend couldn't continue. The Russians were just too seasoned, too good.

The experts forgot to keep one thing in mind though: the Russians were complacent and cocky, and the Americans were lean and hungry. What happened may not make the history books, but it was certainly heralded in the nation's newspapers. The U.S. team upset the Russians and won the gold medal! They were hungry lions, out after their prey.

There's a moral to all this, and its a very important one. In hard times, the fat and sassy get eaten by the lean and hungry.

"Now's the time to worry!"

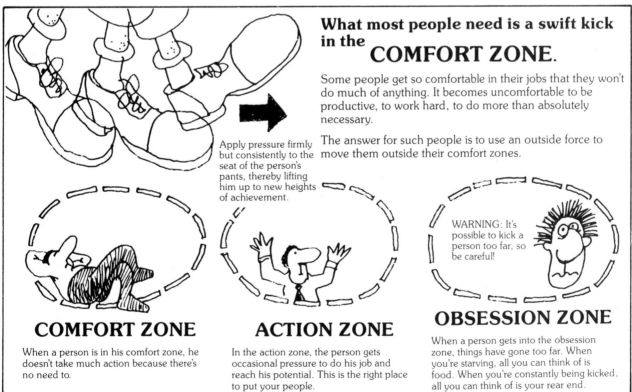

Apply pressure firmly but consistently to the seat of the person's pants, thereby lifting him up to new heights of achievement.

What most people need is a swift kick in the COMFORT ZONE.

Some people get so comfortable in their jobs that they won't do much of anything. It becomes uncomfortable to be productive, to work hard, to do more than absolutely necessary.

The answer for such people is to use an outside force to move them outside their comfort zones.

WARNING: It's possible to kick a person too far, so be careful!

COMFORT ZONE

When a person is in his comfort zone, he doesn't take much action because there's no need to.

ACTION ZONE

In the action zone, the person gets occasional pressure to do his job and reach his potential. This is the right place to put your people.

OBSESSION ZONE

When a person gets into the obsession zone, things have gone too far. When you're starving, all you can think of is food. When you're constantly being kicked, all you can think of is your rear end.

But That's the Way We've Always Done It

"Where our country is in trouble, it is where people have refused to change . . . in the auto industry, where they kept on building big cars, in the savings and loan industry, where they kept on offering low-interest savings accounts. We are in trouble wherever people predicted that past trends would always continue."

Jane Bryant Quinn
Economics Writer

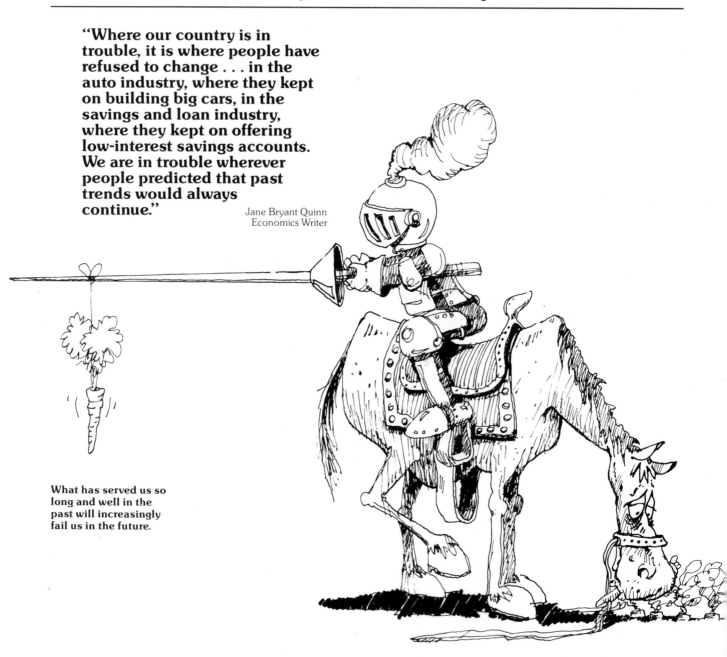

What has served us so long and well in the past will increasingly fail us in the future.

"We've always done it this way."

"We don't question things. Our methods have been proven through years of experience."

"Our methods obviously work. Look at last year's profits."

"Ours is not to reason why. Ours is but to do or die!"

"This system has evolved through many years of hard work. To change now would be a waste."

"What was good enough for me when I started this business is good enough for you now."

The status quo discourages innovation.
The status quo works from the principle of inertia: stationary objects are difficult to get going; moving objects are difficult to stop. Things that are established and moving have an incredible advantage over things that are new.

A good example can be seen in the world economies. Great Britain was really the first country in the world to go through the industrial revolution. The technology and work approach of the entire country changed—and became firmly established. Now the country is in dire need of change to resolve the problems of a harmfully sluggish economy as well as to meet the needs and opportunities of new technology.

Despite the great need, the British are finding it hard to make the change. The status quo weighs on them very heavily.

Now look at the powerful economy of Japan. They are quickly becoming the strongest industrialized nation in the world, in terms of economy. How did they do it? *They didn't have to fight their status quo!* It was destroyed in World War II. After the war they were able to start anew and build a whole new structure.

> **"Even today few businessmen understand that research, to be productive, has to be the 'disorganizer,' the creator of a different future and the enemy of today."**
> Peter Drucker

Nothing Can Be Done

A colleague of mine was once asked to act as a consultant to a major corporation. His assignment was to analyze the information systems of the company and to recommend changes. It was easy for him to see the problems—there were so many. The management approach in the company discouraged innovation and encouraged each

The man started with a simple log.

He built it up to a nice raft.

He added onto it and fixed it up.

Eventually he added a paddle wheel.

"You'd better get something light and fast. There's trouble ahead!"

The longer a person stays with something and the more he invests in it, the less willing he'll be to move to something else—even when it's needed.

Internal consistency is valued more highly than efficient service. Peter's Inversion

person to pull back and protect himself. Job functions were duplicated from department to department.

In fact, my colleague compared the output of the corporation to another, much smaller company in the same area—and showed the corporation officials that the small company was decidedly outperforming the larger one. He then showed them how they could duplicate the small company's performance.

Their response in the end: "I know you're right, but nothing can be done. We can't implement your recommendations. Our entire system is already set up and going."

Too Hard to Fight

Often the status quo is impossible to fight. Those who are part of it have a vested interest in maintaining the past. The answer is *not* to fight it. Instead, wait and watch for these opportunities:

- The status quo fails. When a trusted approach, product, or service fails to produce the old results, often people will be open to new ideas.

- A company or individual starts in a new direction and has no status quo to protect.

- An entirely new enterprise is established.

- A company's key personnel (especially the decision makers) are changed.

- A more competitive opponent poses a serious threat.

Innovation is an important key to success in any business. **The status quo is an enemy that will constantly try to hold us back from tomorrow's business advances.** Managers must create an innovative environment that helps them continually discard the outmoded and unworkable. If they don't, they'll have a difficult time getting to where they want to be.

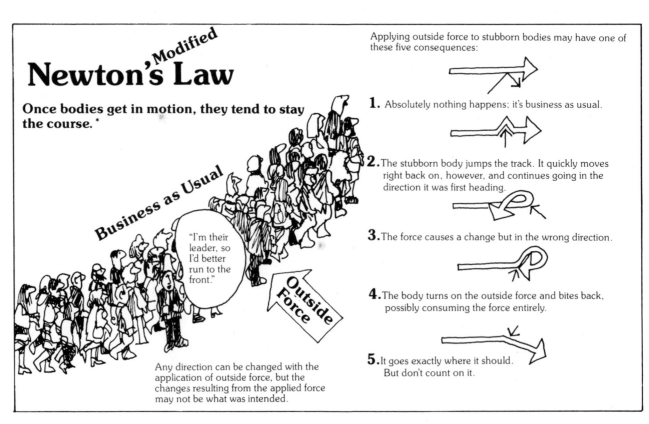

Newton's Modified Law

Once bodies get in motion, they tend to stay the course. *

Business as Usual

"I'm their leader, so I'd better run to the front."

Outside Force

Any direction can be changed with the application of outside force, but the changes resulting from the applied force may not be what was intended.

Applying outside force to stubborn bodies may have one of these five consequences:

1. Absolutely nothing happens; it's business as usual.

2. The stubborn body jumps the track. It quickly moves right back on, however, and continues going in the direction it was first heading.

3. The force causes a change but in the wrong direction.

4. The body turns on the outside force and bites back, possibly consuming the force entirely.

5. It goes exactly where it should. But don't count on it.

* These are human bodies, alone or in a group.

The Constant Called Change

Failing to Adapt

A common problem of many businesses is that they fail to adapt to changing conditions. When everything is going well, it's easy to feel that everything will always go well. It's easy to get complacent.

It's easy to think that the future will be the same as the glorious past. Unfortunately, that's often not the case. The only thing certain about life (other than death and taxes) is *change*. About the only thing that never changes is the fact that there is always change.

Examples can be found all over the place:

- **Ford Motor Company** dominated the industry in its early years. The founders of the company were innovators and pioneers, and they had the vision that was needed to carry Ford through several decades. But the second and third generations weren't as able to adapt to changing circumstances. They held fast to the methods of the past, offering "any color car, as long as it's black." Eventually they lost their first-place standing.

- The **A. C. Gilbert Company** at one time was a major toy company in the United States. It was internationally known for its Erector sets and American Flyer trains. But the company failed to keep pace with the times. When other toy manufacturers were moving into television advertising in the 1950s and 1960s, Gilbert was about three steps behind. When other toy manufacturers were forming and following the trend from model trains to slot-car auto racing sets, Gilbert clung to its American Flyer. In the end, because it failed to adapt adequately, the company folded after nearly sixty years of successful business.

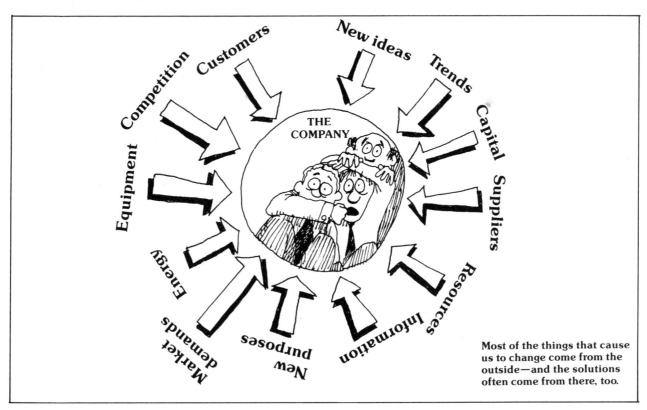

Most of the things that cause us to change come from the outside—and the solutions often come from there, too.

- At one time, **Talon** was the number one zipper in the world. It was used primarily in dresses. Textron acquired the zipper in 1968, and for five or six years thereafter, it was one of Textron's biggest money makers. But the inevitable change came, and Talon didn't change with it. Dress styles changed, and jeans began to supplant dresses. The demand for the Talon zipper dropped dramatically. There wasn't much Textron could do about that. But Textron didn't have anything to replace it. They didn't adapt. They simply lost out.

Outside Solutions

Nothing in life is as certain as change. And nothing about change is as certain as the fact that many people will resist it.

As information and technology explode all around us, change is accelerating. Those who learn to adjust and make the necessary changes will survive. The others, who continue to maintain the status quo and react as they always have, may find themselves failing at an increasing rate.

When it comes time to make a change, what should people do? How can they find the right change for the right time?

People often respond to a need for change by looking inside themselves. They think and ponder and try to "figure things out" from their internal point of view. That's the macho instinct at work: "I can handle things all by myself."

That approach, though, often isn't the best one. **The critical solution to problems is often found outside ourselves.** Some examples:

- The chameleon and the army tank share the same problem: as they move into a new environment, they want to remain unseen. The answer is camouflage—they change on the outside to match the environment.

- The doctors in a clinic were wasting too much time looking up patient data. It was hurting their profits. They found the solution outside themselves, in computer technology. They put a terminal in each patient room and found the data at their fingertips.

- An alcoholic wanted to change but couldn't. He found his solution outside himself, in associating with other alcoholics who also wanted to change.

- An artist was having trouble selling his work. His solution was outside, in the buyers. He found they didn't want great works of art but cute things to hang on their walls.

- When a company finds itself with cash-flow problems, it will often look inside for solutions: "Let's cut here and trim here." Sometimes that works, but often the best solution is outside. They can go to a banker and get the cash to tide them over.

- When a company wants to beat tough competition, it can sometimes succeed by looking outside. Management can cut their prices in the marketplace. And they can go outside for better equipment and newer technology, thus increasing their productivity.

- When a lion is hungry, it doesn't look inside for a solution. It goes outside, into the larger environment, and finds a buffalo to eat.

Problems invariably come to every manager and every company. And the natural tendency is to look inside for solutions. Those solutions, however, can increasingly be found on the outside, but they'll be found only by those who look.

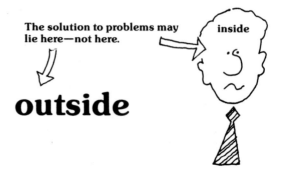

The solution to problems may lie here—not here.

inside

outside

Flexibility

Aaron's Bodyworks

Aaron was the president of an android-making business. He made wonderful bodies—everyone wanted one. But then he decided to specialize. A whole body was kind of awkward, clunky. But there was one part of the body he really liked: the hand. It was a marvel of engineering. All those little bones working so well together. The thumb opposing the other digits. Aaron got excited just thinking about the hand!

So he went into the hand business. "Specialization is the thing!" he exulted to his board of directors. "We'll become the hand capital of the world!"

Then he told them all the things hands were good for:

- Picking up things
- Shaking other hands
- Getting attention at meetings
- Asking to go to the bathroom

"But what about eyes?" asked one of the board members.

"Well, I guess we could also make an occasional eye," Aaron said. "But nothing else. After all, with a skilled hand and a watchful eye, what else do you need?"

So the company went to work. It produced the best hands in the galaxy, with an occasional eye. Business boomed. Whenever people wanted an extra hand, they knew just where to go: straight to Aaron's Bodyworks.

As their profits grew, so did their expertise. They started making purple hands, striped hands, and hands with orange fingernails. They made hands that had the grip of a vise and hands that could hold a baby's finger gently.

It was the success story of the twenty-first century. Even *Fortune* magazine featured the company on its cover: "Hand Firm Shakes Out Big Bucks."

Hand Sales Sag

Then one day a man developed a hand with a foot attached. "Hey, these are much more versatile," the consumers said. "With a foot attached, the hand can get around."

Aaron scoffed. "Hands are the thing," he said. Some tried to change his mind, but he wouldn't

Aaron's Bodyworks was geared to only one product. They had no room for diversity.

"Our productivity is running at an all-time high."

listen. And when his company went into receivership, no one raised a hand to help him.

Tomorrow's successful organization will have a diversity of function in order to have a flexibility of operation. It will do several things well so that it can move in any of several directions if the business climate dictates change.

The time to prepare for tomorrow's competitive approach is today. Managers need to be willing to

- Make changes when needed

- Take advantage of new markets

- Learn how to spot danger on the horizon—and avoid it

- Keep up on new knowledge—and take advantage of it

CAD-CAM

The management approach made possible by computers gives us a good example. With a method called CAD-CAM (computer-aided design-computer-aided manufacturing), everything in a plant is tied together through a computer system. A designer can create a widget on his computer, then transfer the design to another computer. The second computer can then drive a machine that will actually start producing the widget.

The next day, the designer can create a womblit on his computer and transfer it. The second computer can then oversee the production of the womblits.

CAD-CAM is the driving force behind the factory of the future. The organization that can produce with CAD-CAM must be flexible and adaptable to new systems, approaches, and technology.

Stuck Stiff

Many management approaches are effective when they're first begun. They may work for

many years. But the day will likely come when they'll be outmoded. Then what happens? If the company is flexible, it will change its approach. And survive. But if the company is too rigid, it may go the way of the buggy whip and the sundial. The company may wish to change but be utterly unable to; then rigidity can kill.

A friend of mine once worked for a book publisher. The publishing company did well in its niche. But as times changed, the things that people were interested in began to change. Women became more interested in their basic rights; men became interested in things other than the climb up the corporate ladder. But the publishing company was rigid. It had one kind of approach to publishing books and only one. It was unable to change with the times. It didn't have the diversity and flexibility it needed to survive and prosper.

An Orchestra

Picture a professional orchestra. Each person has his own instrument, which he can play to perfection. The conductor pulls all the sounds together—the violins, the flutes, the drums—until the unified effort produces beautiful music. The diversity of function is orchestrated into a unity of operation. That diversity gives the orchestra needed flexibility: if the orchestra choose to, they can perform Beethoven or Bacharach, the Beatles or Brahms.

The future belongs to the flexible.

"I'm tired of hearing about how good the Japanese are! Our admiration and fear are fogging up our eyesight. We are blinded in seeing their strengths and weaknesses.

"They are an extremely homogenous workforce that has built an economic giant mostly by improving on our genius. That genius in us comes from our diversity. A diversity we often seemed obsessed in killing by hammering it into a rigid conformity.

"Our problem isn't just Japan's productivity, but our inability to turn our natural diversity into an economic advantage."

Overspecializing on Specialists

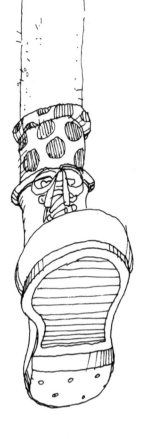

- Never ask only a barber if you need a haircut.

- Never ask only a surgeon if it should be removed.

- Never ask only a banker if honesty is a virtue.

- Never ask only an entomologist about termites in your basement.

- Never ask only a comptroller for more petty cash.

- Never ask only a salesperson if you really need it.

- Never ask only a friend how you look.

If you depend solely on specialists for your guidance, tomorrow will come and stomp on your head.

Our society is infected with too many specialists, each proclaiming that his narrow view is the total answer. Their goal is for expert systems or interface planners or statistical mechanics or genealogical tracers to rule the world.

There is power in specialization. By narrowing your effort to some obscure niche in society, you can become the best, if only because no one else knows what you're talking about. It's also safe there because little boxed worlds are predictable and controllable.

But if you depend on the specialists, you get specialized answers. Everyone wants an expert brain surgeon if a tumor's up there. But what if it isn't, or what if another approach besides surgery is possible for treating the tumor. I'm not saying specialists aren't valuable or even critical at times, but someone has got to be seeing the stars while all the others are looking at the ground.

Every organization needs a generalist or two to see the relationship between the parts. And to look out for the big foot.

"We had better move! That's a helluva big foot!"

"My shoes are made of genuine Naugahyde."

"Most paper clips are thrown away, you know."

"Many grasses are edible."

"Isn't that a plagioclase feldspar rock by your hand?"

"This is the largest buchitiata beetle I've ever seen."

Give a small boy a hammer, and he will find that everything he encounters needs pounding.

Kaplan's Law

Saving for Tomorrow

Eating Tomorrow's Potatoes

A farmer in Idaho recently fell on hard times. He had gone to the bank and borrowed enough money to get him through the year, which is standard procedure—but when he sold his crop at the end of the summer, he was way short. The bank was getting anxious, and they started to put on the pressure. They finally got so much money from him that he wasn't sure how his family would make it through the winter.

October came and went. November. December. Finally all the family's money and food were gone, and they were hungry. The farmer went to the only place he could go. He had a cellar full of seed potatoes, the potatoes he was going to use to plant next year's crop. He went down to the cellar and got a bushel of potatoes. "I'll get just this much," he said. "That won't hurt."

A few days later his family was hungry again. "I'll get just a few more," he told himself.

By the time spring came and it was time to plant a new crop, the seed potatoes were all gone. By giving in to short-term pressures, the farmer had destroyed his future. He had eaten tomorrow's potatoes today, so when tomorrow came, he had nothing left.

Managers must be careful that they don't let the present pressure destroy the future possibilities.

Sometimes we sacrifice our tomorrows for today's needs.

Sacrificing Tomorrow for Today

Consider the manager who's under pressure to produce. He's getting demands from all sides: the investors and stockholders, his bosses, the profit-sharing subordinates. The demand is for more profits, immediate gains. Finally the pressure gets to him, and he caves in: He sacrifices tomorrow for relief today. He takes money away from research and development of ideas. He cuts down on the number of employees. He cuts down on the quality of materials. He stops spending money to train his people. The company shows a profit immediately. But what's going to happen tomorrow?

Shrinking Grasslands

The desert dwellers in Africa are making a similar mistake. The grasslands that provide food for cattle, shelter for game, and materials for fire and shelter are limited, and the people who need the grasslands are destroying them. Without thought of reseeding, cultivating, or preserving, they cut the vegetation for fires or feed it to their cattle. In doing so, they are meeting today's need—but they are destroying their future.

Scavenging Planes

A squadron of the U.S. Air Force once got low on parts for their planes. They wanted to keep their planes in the air, so they started scavenging parts from other planes. A part here, a part there—soon they had more planes downed through scavenged parts than they had in the air.

Then they were ordered into the air for a surprise drill. Only three planes could make it up. The squadron had ruined their tomorrow for their today.

If we don't save anything for tomorrow, there will be no tomorrow.

Note: If you want to read "seed corn" for "potatoes" in the above story, you may. You'll find the lesson is the same.

Too often managers make the mistake of counting what they need to invest in their future as profit. It should not be counted as profit but as expenses—the money that needs to be invested in new people, markets, equipment, etc., to have a productive future.

From Stagnant to Applied Knowledge

An important key to innovation in a company is to apply new knowledge you acquire, as you obtain it, rather than to simply reapply the old knowledge over and over again. The distinction is a crucial one. **Failure to effectively apply newly acquired knowledge is one key cause of productivity loss.**

And, what's worse, failure to apply old knowledge in new ways will lead to your company being left in the dust by competitors! For progress it's essential to take what you already know and make it do new things for you. If your company or group isn't doing that, be assured that someone else is—and their approach will eventually make yours obsolete.

Don't let knowledge stagnate.

Transistors and Soap

In the early 1950s, Western Electric had the rights to the transistor, but they weren't doing much with it. They weren't applying what they had. In 1953, they sold those rights to Sony for a mere $25,000. That one little investment by Sony became the basis of a multibillion-dollar industry.

Shortly after World War II, the top management of a soap products company considered developing a home laundry detergent. Detergents were available for industrial use, but none had been developed for home use. As the management thought about it, they decided not to move into the home market. They chose not to apply their knowledge in new ways.

At the same time, another soap manufacturer, this one much smaller, decided to adapt their knowledge to the new potential market. It took two years to come up with an acceptable product—but the smaller company then quickly passed up its big brother in sales and took the major share of the market for the next decade. They did all this through applying what they already knew in a new way.

Sailing Ships and Steamers

Another example can be seen in the shipping industry. When steamships were first introduced, they were slow and unreliable, even though the technology had definite potential. But rather than seek to perfect steamships, the old shipmakers sought to further improve their sailing ships. They made them faster and sleeker than ever, trying to forever eliminate the menace of the steamships.

Their lack of foresight proved to be their undoing. As the knowledge about steam power was applied in ever-new ways, the steamship became the quickest and most economical way of transporting by water. By failing to apply new knowledge in new ways, the sailing-ship makers eventually drove themselves out of business.

A Few Ideas

Innovation is the application of present knowledge for future productivity. Here are some ways to acquire and apply new ideas:

- Scale down the size of your tests of new ideas. Gamble a little to see if they work. You can gamble a little many times, but a lot only once or twice.

- Go outside your organization to find new ideas. When you get too committed to your own operations and procedures, you may become blind to great ideas that are close by.

- Deliberately bring in new people and their accompanying points of view. New blood will help generate new ideas.

- Implement an organization-wide philosophy: "If you can find a better way to do this, we want to hear about it."

- Reward big efforts with big benefits. This is a simple motivational tool that works. Let your workers know that if they come up with workable innovations, they'll be rewarded for their ideas.

- Create a place where innovators will be safe. Let creative people do what they know best: take knowledge and turn it into a newly applied benefit.

- Get some customers in a room, and find out what they want from you, what they don't want, and what they hate. If you listen with an open mind, this can be very revealing.

- Let your best people take a sabbatical. They may came back with a valuable new orientation.

- Create an atmosphere where you can teach one another. It's surprising how much your people know and can share with their co-workers (and bosses).

- Break each department down into "families." A group that's too large automatically seems to discourage innovation.

- A lot of ideas to choose from tends to produce an increase in success. Encourage a lot of ideas from all directions.

- Create a way to share information you're picking up from magazines, books, lectures, new products, and so forth.

Note: The longer something just sits, the harder it is to use, like a muscle that isn't used and gradually atrophies. The same is true of ideas and people.

Throwing Your Competition

Using a Little Judo

The judo expert has a good idea when it comes to dealing with competition. Instead of trying to fight them, he joins them. And in the process he beats them.

A judo expert will never get into a tug-of-war with his opponents. Instead he'll use his opponents' force against them. When the opponents use force, they're off balance, and their own weight sends them to the mat.

The competition's coming at you? Great! Don't try to push them back. Let them build momentum. Then find their weakness, and trip them!

The best way to overcome competition is to find their strengths. Find their weaknesses. **Then pit your strengths against their weaknesses.**

To do that, a manager has to be very aware of what the competition's up to. He'll need to get out of his cocoon and observe and listen to what's going on.

In our society, too much time is spent worrying about what the competition's up to—and too little scouting them out.

Scouting Out Your Competition

A good football coach doesn't make this mistake. He attends his opponents' games. He watches films of what they did. Then, if they're best at defending a ground game, he'll come at them with an air game. If they're best at air games, he puts in his ground game. They can't do everything equally well. So the coach finds their weaknesses and uses it against them.

Exporting Radios to Japan

General Electric used this approach with their "value engineering" program. The competition was charging a certain amount for their transistor radios—and GE decided to undercut them. They did it by breaking their radios down to all their parts and examining the costs of producing every part; they considered the transistors, the speakers, the dials, the casing, the cost of purchasing, the cost of putting the parts together, the cost of shipping—everything. They found the places where they were spending too much. They found the redundancies in their process.

And it worked. Their costs dropped so much that they were soon able to export their radios to *Japan!* (That was until the Japanese caught on and started doing it back.)

P.S. If your competition is any good, they'll do the same thing right back to you.

Even though your opponent may be imposing and strong . . .

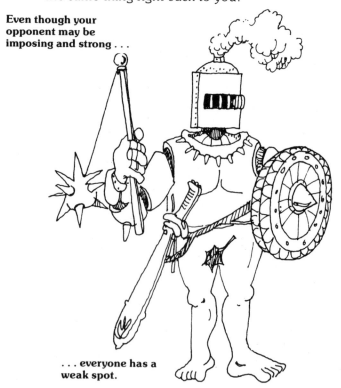

. . . everyone has a weak spot.

"My football team was one of the losers in the conference. But we decided one day that we were going to whip the number one team, just to build back our pride. We visited their games and watched films hours on end. Finally we saw their weak point. When we started to play, we attacked that one point, battering it time after time. They were a strong team, but not at that point of weakness. We won the game!"

Coach of a university football team

Note: You'd better know a lot about your own strengths and weaknesses before you try this. The best approach is to get an outsider to take a look at your company. You're too close to see it clearly.

Three Ways to Grow

Deadly Decision

At one point Montgomery Ward was a vital, growing firm. Then its management determined a new policy: even though there was still room for growth, they decided to be cautious, to hold the company to its present size, to refuse to grow anymore.

That decision was deadly. The company became weaker and weaker until finally it was bought out by a conglomerate.

Compare Ward's fate with that of Sears. Sears is the same kind of store, selling basically the same kind of merchandise. But its management was aggressive in their growth strategy, and by the early 1980s Sears was one of the top two retailers in the nation.

It's impossible for a company to stand still. It must either grow or die. Companies are in the same situation as the swimmer out in the lake. The swimmer must progress across the water or die. He can dog-paddle for a while, but he can't keep that up indefinitely. That's good only for the moment, while he takes stock of his situation and decides where to go next. But it's the going that keeps him alive. It's sink or swim, both for swimmers and for companies.

There are many different ways an organization can grow: knowledge, skills, efficiency, productivity, location, finances, etc.

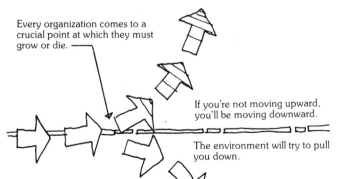

Every organization comes to a crucial point at which they must grow or die.

If you're not moving upward, you'll be moving downward.

The environment will try to pull you down.

How to Grow

Companies can grow in three different ways, often in the sequence listed:

1 SIZE

There is a limit to how big you can grow physically.

As you grow, there will be tremendous pressures trying to hold you back.

Growth is limited by the resources available.

Many organizations can grow in physical size, but the time comes when they're limited by their basic nature. A hummingbird can't ever grow larger than a hummingbird. A whale can grow much larger—but never beyond the natural maximum for a whale.

In the same way, a consulting firm can experience growth in size. A car manufacturer can do the same. But if the consulting firm tried to become as large as the manufacturer, it would have outgrown itself. Each organization can grow only as large as its nature will allow.

Limiting factors: setting, resources, people, niche, markets, and so forth.

2 REPLICATION

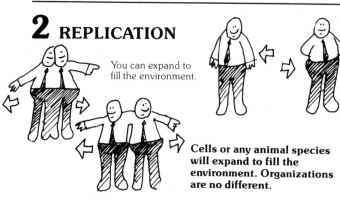

You can expand to fill the environment.

Cells or any animal species will expand to fill the environment. Organizations are no different.

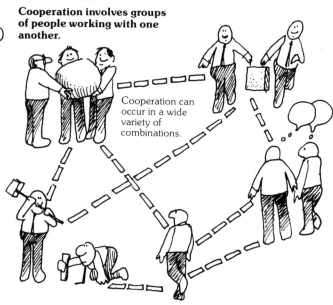

Cooperation involves groups of people working with one another.

Cooperation can occur in a wide variety of combinations.

If an organization can no longer grow in size, it can still grow through replication. It can make another one of itself. This method has its limits, too. Replication is limited by the environment. Get too many deer in one area, and they'll starve. Get too many units of the same company in one area, and many of them will die.

Examples of replication: A company may choose to establish franchises. It can reproduce itself over and over, until the environment is filled—within the limits of what the environment will sustain.

Or the company can build regional offices in different cities. Or repeat the same kind of department within the company. Or buy another company with similar functions but leave the new company autonomous.

3 COOPERATION

Through cooperation, a corporation can form relationships with others. That relationship can bring growth to all involved. A good example is seen in a family. A woman may have certain capabilities. A man may have others. By joining together in marriage, then cooperating, they both can grow—economically, socially, emotionally, and intellectually. Like the other forms of growth, cooperation also has limits. The limits: the perceptions of those involved. You can grow through cooperation with another as much as you think you can.

We've all seen cooperation at work. A manufacturer, distributor, and retailer all cooperate to reach a common goal of selling the product. By cooperating with each other, all may grow bigger.

A client, an advertising agency, and a magazine may all cooperate to tell people about a product or service.

Parents, a principal, a teacher, and a group of kids may all cooperate to help children learn in school.

Choose Your Growth

Since every corporation must either grow or die, you should have a set plan for growth. **The important thing is to choose the kind of growth that is best for you.** Only then will you be able to take the proper steps as you move along from year to year.

Remember that growth isn't enough. It must be the right kind. Peter Drucker gave some wise advice. He said in essence:

In analyzing the growth you're experiencing, the crucial thing is to be able to tell the difference between fat and cancer and muscle.

Organizations can grow faster than their brains can manage them in relation to their environment and to their own physiology. When this occurs, they are an endangered species.
Bronto Saurus Principle

How Do I Know How Productive We Are?

The more you keep track of where your profit comes from, the more profit you'll usually get. Once you know where you are, you'll know better where to do your work. You'll know what's working well and what isn't. From there it's an easy step to greater productivity.

Using a Map

If you want to take a journey to another city, one you've never visited before, you'll most likely need a map. But the map will be utterly worthless unless you take a vital first step: find out where you presently are on the map. Once you know your present position, you'll be able to move out from there.

The same is true in business. If you don't know where you are now, there's no way you'll be able to reach your goals. The first step to improvement is adequate evaluation of current circumstances.

Which Financial Statement?

Many organizations use a financial statement as their measure of profits and productivity. But there is a problem with that approach. For starters, which financial statement do you work from? Do you use the one

- You sent the stockholders?

- You created for that loan?

- The IRS saw?

- You used in trying to make that acquisition?

Do you use the monthly reports? the quarterly reports? the annual reports? the five-year projection?

Something to Try

If financial statements don't provide a good accounting method, what does? Here's an approach to try. Figure out what it costs to produce one unit of product or service in your business. Once you know that information, you have a basis for evaluating your work.

Examples:

- An interior design firm has been in business for twelve years—and they're in deep financial trouble. Their problem is that they've never computed their unit-of-production costs. What do they produce? Designs. And a unit of production would be one contract with one client. By figuring out what each unit costs and by figuring out what they get from it, they'll be able to see where both their money and their time are going.

- For a bank, a unit of production is a loan. One bank that's having trouble needs to figure out its unit of production. The manager will find that he has too many small loans. It takes as much time to process a small loan as it does to process a large one. The bank can improve its productivity by making more large loans.

- A company like McDonald's, the fast-food chain, has a unit of production in the form of one transaction. It takes virtually as long to process a transaction for a single person as it does for an entire family. McDonald's management has recognized this, and they've boosted their productivity by advertising that McDonald's is a family-oriented place.

- For a father or mother, a unit of production might be getting one child off to school in the morning or one batch of wash completed or one meal prepared.

- For an entomologist, a unit of production might be one butterfly mounted on a board, with an accompanying description written underneath.

- For a baker, a unit of production might be one 5-pound bag of flour transformed into cookies and cakes.

Note: Along the various channels of production in a given company, each person will have a different goal. But to be productive, each person's goal must be consistent with the overall company goal. For example, a welder in a car factory may see a perfect weld as one unit of production; that leads to the factory's final goal of a finished car as a unit of production.

- Even a service organization can figure units of production. First, they need to state their goals simply and clearly and devise a way to measure their success. Once that's done, they'll be able to proceed. With a church, for example, a key goal might be to get the people into the building on Sunday. One person attending can be defined as one unit of production. As more and more people attend, productivity has climbed.

Ask These Questions

To use this approach for yourself, ask these questions. Think carefully about the answers.

1. What is our unit or units of production?

2. Is our system—and is our way of accounting for our production—simple? Can everyone involved use it?

3. What is the cost per unit of production?

4. What are our past successes and failures, in terms of units of production?

5. Do we have a way to redefine our unit of production if we need to?

6. Who decides the value of one unit of production?

7. In what ways can we increase the value of the unit of production while decreasing its costs?

8. Are we presently using any of these methods?

9. What is the competition doing? What do they count as a unit of production?

"Not long ago I spoke with the owner-manager of a unionized Michigan furniture factory. He awards his workers with a weekly bonus, which varies with the 'labor content' of the cabinets produced during the week. The less labor time per cabinet, the bigger the bonus. The system is so successful that workers actually tell managers when they think a new employee is not good enough to stay on the payroll.

"Productivity sharing has a great advantage over profit sharing. Profits depend upon many factors over which workers have no control. But workers have a lot of control over their own productivity. They can see when their efforts pay off. Someone else's mistakes do not offset their successes."

Economist Lester C. Thurow,
writing in *INC.* magazine

Key unit of production

⬇

A given amount of time in the air with a paying customer

Once you know your key unit of production, you can ask the kinds of questions that will increase productivity.

Use nonunion help?

Longer trips and charge more?

How can we make it more fun and exciting?

Night flying? More trips?

TV ads? Radio?

How can I lower my propane costs? Can I heat with cheaper fuel?

Can I pay the pilot according to the number of flights he takes?

Helium? Hydrogen?

Dangerous?

What's the most I can make per trip?

Insurance?

Can I increase the number of balloons?

Can I increase the size of the balloon to hold more people?

Use balloons to advertise?

How can I get a continuous supply of people who want to go up?

Is the customer willing to pay more?

What makes a customer come back?

Can I offer a group rate to attract more customers?

Bright colors for balloons?

Note: People inherently need to measure themselves. But it's surprising what some choose as the unit of production: the amount of paper on the desk, the hours worked, the time on the road, gross income, numbers of report pages, number of long-distance calls, number of full file cabinets. Productivity will never increase unless the right unit of production is selected.

Learning from the Most Productive People in the World

The reasons for the farmer's productivity are all around him. He's so productive that even the Japanese can't match him. In fact, one of their biggest imports from the United States is the farmer's output.

If the farmer's methods could be transferred to other forms of business, we'd become more productive and prosperous than we've ever dreamed of.

Support equipment

The farmer gets as much support equipment as he possibly can.

The farmer has much more support equipment than other typical U.S. workers.

New products

When a new product (or process) is proven, the farmer adopts it quickly.

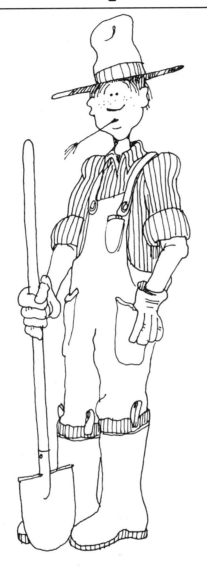

Training

The farmer takes the vital opportunity to learn by doing.

Notice how the farmer dresses for success!

Application of knowledge

When a useful new idea comes along, the farmer is quick to try it.

Attitudes and beliefs

Farmers can see the relationship between what they do (or don't do) and the results they get.

Compare the farmer's approach with that of the white-collar worker.

Perhaps few people are more productive than the U.S. farmer. Yearly, fewer and fewer farmers produce more and more food. The farmer seems to be the essence of productivity. Just a small number of them grow enough food to feed a good portion of the world. How do they do it? The answers are informative for everyone interested in productivity, no matter what the field.

• **Support equipment.** A recent newspaper story contained the following facts: "The average farmer has about $150,000 worth of 'support equipment' to help accomplish his tasks. The average factory worker has about $50,000 in support equipment. The average white-collar worker has about $2,000 worth." With that kind of investment in his work, is it any wonder the farmer has a high level of productivity?

As Rodger Sneed, chicken farmer, says, "I can't afford NOT to have the best and latest equipment and stock. If I don't, I'm dead." How many office or factory managers feel that way?

Farmers have got their problems too. Some of their productivity has been gained at the expense of tomorrow. The pressures of the present have reduced the fertility of the soil and the needed investment in the new equipment and processes.

- **Training.** Unlike many other fields of endeavor, farmers learn their jobs almost strictly by doing. Even those who go to college learn through a hands-on approach. When a farmer has to learn a new method, he goes out and tries it. Compare his experience with that of most white-collar workers, who have learned their trade in a classroom setting.

- **New products.** Farmers are constantly adopting new and more efficient products and processes. For example, in 1945 it took fourteen weeks to get a chicken from the egg to a salable size. With breeding and a controlled environment, farmers have been able to cut that fourteen weeks down to seven and a half. Another example: The average dairy herd in the United States is presently only half the size it was in 1950. Yet it produces more milk!

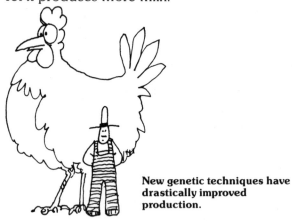

New genetic techniques have drastically improved production.

- **Application of knowledge.** The farming community has one central purpose: to improve productivity. Because of that, support people, from county agents to sellers of farm products, are in the business of selling information. Part of the overall farming consciousness is an open-mindedness to new ideas and techniques: "If you can prove it will improve my production, I'll buy it." Because of farmers' willingness to apply new ideas, the time that elapses from idea to proven practical application to a product in the hands of the farmer is much shorter than in most other systems.

- **Attitudes and beliefs.** Farmers' attitudes and beliefs are very conducive to productivity. They love their work: "I can't see myself doing anything else," says the farmer.

They can *see* the correlation between what they do or don't do and the results they get.

They learn key principles and learn how to apply them in their work. Examples of such principles: "The law of the harvest always works. If you plant and fertilize and water, the plants will come up." "The future is always better when we invest in it."

Too Productive for Their Own Good

The result of the farmer's situation is that his productivity (rate of output per units of input) has increased by twenty-five percent in the past fifteen years. The farmer has become so productive that three percent of the U.S. population is feeding the remaining ninety-seven percent—plus a good portion of the rest of the world.

It's true that the farmer is having a difficult time nowadays. How can this be? The answer most likely lies in the system the farmer has to work in. The farmer is too productive for his own good! He needs to learn to be as productive in marketing as he is in production. Having worked in both areas, I can see that both farming and marketing involve the same basic concepts. The farmer must simply learn to apply the concepts he already knows to a new area.

In productivity, the farmer is head and shoulders above any other segment in our economy—or any other economy in the world. He produces at a higher rate than the system can assimilate. It would be interesting to transfer the farmer's mentality to the rest of society, just to see how productive everyone could be!

Thirty-nine Proven Principles for Increasing Productivity

As I gathered information for this book, I talked to a lot of different people and visited a lot of different organizations. I wanted to find out exactly what lies behind high productivity. I was surprised at what I found: **The principles for productivity are the same whether you're in a family, a ball team, a high school, a company, or a service organization.**

A family works on basic organizational principles.

Family

A football team is very different from a family—but it works by the same principles.

Football Team

Company

A company must work by the same principles as a family and a football team.

Compartmentalization

We do ourselves a disservice when we try to treat a business organization as different from other kinds of organizations. We see a football team succeeding, and we say, "Well, that coach has a good thing going, but that would never work in my office." We see a family accomplish a great deal by working together, and we say, "That would never work in my shop. Things are different there."

Yes, things *are* different at the office and at the shop. But people are the same everywhere. And what motivates people in one setting usually motivates in another setting. It's inaccurate to try to put different organizations in different compartments.

So what makes different organizations work?

Here's a partial list of the ideas others shared:

- Make decisions based on the values of the organization.

- Have a consistent leadership style and philosophy.

- Live the Golden Rule, doing to others as you'd have them do to you.

- Teach others to visualize their potential and the potential of the group.

- Put the right person in the right job.

- Don't underestimate the abilities of the worker.

- Give constant support, but at the same time challenge people to step out of their comfort zone and stretch themselves.

- Treat failures as learning experiences leading to success.

- Let managers have a "high degree of engagement" with their workers.

- Have goals and values that all workers can agree with.

- Encourage managers to be human—even to smile occasionally!

- Teach others to give away their jobs: encourage them to teach others what they know.

- Set up a system that covers all the bases. Put specific people in charge of specific tasks, and outline the responsibilities clearly.

- Make people responsible for results, not for methods.
- Encourage the establishment of teams. The success of the individual will contribute to the success of the team, which will contribute to the success of the company.
- Simplify rather than complicate.
- Don't put a limit on achievement.
- Make sure that everyone feels important and necessary to the success of the group.
- Give rewards for accomplishments.
- Have a bias toward action.
- Keep a lean staff.
- Maintain constant contact with the customer.
- Encourage entrepreneurship within the company.
- Give workers the information they need to do their job.
- Let employees participate in important decisions.
- Be flexible.
- Avoid bad management practices, including
  —accumulation of paperwork
  —lack of setting priorities
  —lack of delegation
  —procrastination
  —outdated procedures and policies
- Keep equipment up to date.
- Provide employees with adequate supplies.
- Let workers keep up to date in their field.
- Establish a business climate conducive to productivity.
- Maintain a work climate conducive to innovation.
- Give workers adequate training.
- Have a system for monitoring and assessing worker performance.
- Have the manager surround himself with highly competent people.
- Let the worker's need to improve come from within, rather than from without.
- Help each worker establish his own game plan.
- Help each worker understand what he must sacrifice to reach his goal.
- Allow a weekly meeting of employees with no management present. There the employees can express appreciation and learn to support one another.

Learn from Life

One thing we learn from all this is that each of us has tremendous experience in productivity. We almost pick it up automatically, just from being alive. What does it take to build a productive business? The same thing it takes to build a productive family or football team or club or church group.

Often we hesitate to transfer our success from our private lives into our business circles. But nothing could make more sense. An organization is an organization—no matter what its purpose is—as long as it's composed of people.

If you can see what works in one organization, find out the underlying principle. Then apply that principle in other organizations you're concerned with. Chances are you'll have success there too.

"A society that uses people partly or perversely is underproductive. A society that finds ways to involve everybody fully becomes super productive."
Richard Cornvelle

The Dangerous Quality of Poor Organizations

Denton The king

Marion The sidekick

Mel The masochist

Loni The worker

Jan The perfectionist

Wes & Bill The grovelers

Kevin The bouncee

Carlos The bouncer

Jim The sleeper

Fritz The reader

The poor organization is one that drains, one that gives back less than you put in. **Here's what a draining organization comes down to:**

- A situation where every person is out for himself

- An organization where each worker selfishly considers only his own needs

- A situation where the whole is less than the sum of the parts

- An organization where the needs of the individual are different from the needs of the organization, and little or no effort is made to reconcile those needs

- A social structure that takes more than it gives

- A relationship that sucks energy from all involved

- A situation where the individual benefits only at the expense of the organization, and vice versa.

Note: The sad thing about this kind of organization is that it's usually created by the negative expression of real talents. If those talents were properly channeled, the organization might work.

Do any of these sound familiar?

- "My partner doesn't give me any credit for having a brain in my head. Whenever I start to express an opinion, he just laughs my idea away."

- "Every time I leave for work, I can feel my stomach slowly tie itself into a knot and then jump around inside. It lasts all day and halfway into the evening. I often wonder if it's worth it."

- "That store has to be the worst place anywhere. If it weren't the only place in town that sells what I want, I'd never go there, it's such a hassle."

- "My boss is a complete turkey. I think his brain died about two years ago. And his ears are permanently plugged."

- "It's survival that's at stake in this job. You keep your mouth shut and do what you're told. You don't ask questions, and you don't make waves."

Some organizations give back much less than is put in. When that's the case, it would often be better not to belong to them at all.

Those who stick with these destructive organizations soon smell the scent of death in the air. Draining organizations can lead to death in many ways:

- Death of ideas

- Death of opportunity

- Death of joy to be a part of it

- Death of the workers' health

- Sometimes death to the workers themselves

- Eventually death to the organization

(Don't forget that a few perverse workers—who couldn't possibly survive anywhere else—will thrive in this destructive environment.)

How to Recognize Draining Organizations

This kind of organization is easy to identify. Here are the identifying features of draining organizations, given in the order in which they usually appear:

1. **Isolation.** Every man and woman watches out for himself or herself. Management sees things from only one point of view. Everyone lives in his own little cubicle, with no sharing of ideas or goals.

2. **Survival.** Just surviving is the dominant motivation for all who work with the organization. "I just want to find a corner away from the wind." Everyone has a common goal to not make waves or choices—especially if there's risk involved.

3. **Domination.** Just a few people rule the organization. They each see it as their own personal domain; it's a machine created to serve their needs.

4. **Sterility.** All the capable people who work for the organization either dry up or move away. The ground the organization is built on is sterile, unable to give life to new ideas or approaches. Maintaining the status quo is the prime reason for existing.

5. **Closure.** The outside is viewed as a threat. As time passes, reality is viewed as existing only inside the organization; the outside is no longer considered part of the real world.

The Mysterious Quality of Great Organizations

Have you ever noticed these kinds of differences?

- The members of Family One are always complaining at one another. Things never seem to go right, and they never seem able to solve their problems.

  In Family Two the members pull together and are supportive of one another. They have problems too, but they seem able to solve them each time.

- Employees in Company One are constantly expressing dissatisfaction and resentment about the company.

  Company Two is in exactly the same business, in virtually the same location. But their productivity goes up year after year. And the employees actually seem happy to be there!

- Jennifer hates to go to school every day, even though she's bright and likes to read.

  Alan, who goes to the same school but has a different teacher and a different class, loves to go. His teacher is able to motivate even the least interested students into doing good work.

- Football Team One is on a super losing streak. The players have the talent and experience, but they just can't get it together.

  Football Team Two doesn't have quite the same quality players as Team One, but Team Two can't be beat this year.

What is it that all these successes have in common? **Organizations that consistently perform well have a critical factor called SYNERGY.** Synergy means that the sum of the parts is greater than the parts taken individually. A synergistic organization is always adding, building, giving, growing. Draining organizations don't have this quality. They are always taking, destroying, tearing down, eventually dying.

A few examples of synergy:

- A painting is more than a canvas and some paints. If done right, it will give you an emotional experience. That's synergy.

- The metal alloy of chrome, nickel, and steel is much stronger than any of these metals alone. That's synergy.

- The Egyptian plover cleans the crocodile's teeth, helping the crocodile be healthier and giving the plover a free meal. That's synergy.

- An orchestra does more than bring together the strings and the brass instruments and the percussion instruments. It combines the sounds of all the instruments in a musical pattern that's greater than any of the individual parts. That's synergy!

Keys to Synergy

The person or organization hoping to build synergy must find the right keys, preferably developed in the order given below:

- **Correlation.** Make sure the needs of the individual and the organization correlate with each other. Make sure they align. The member must get more of what he wants by belonging than by not belonging.

- **Communication.** All involved must share their vision of what the interrelationship can do for them. Each must see the benefits and how they can be attained. It this cannot be done a synergistic organization will never develop.

- **Growth and development.** This must be the goal of all involved. Each member needs to take pride in his own job, as well as in the work of others.

- **Fertility.** The synergistic organization will be an environment thirsting for new ideas and opportunities. It will allow its members the safety to make mistakes.

- **Open.** The organization will be open to input from outside. It will be open to new people, new ideas, new goals, new resources.

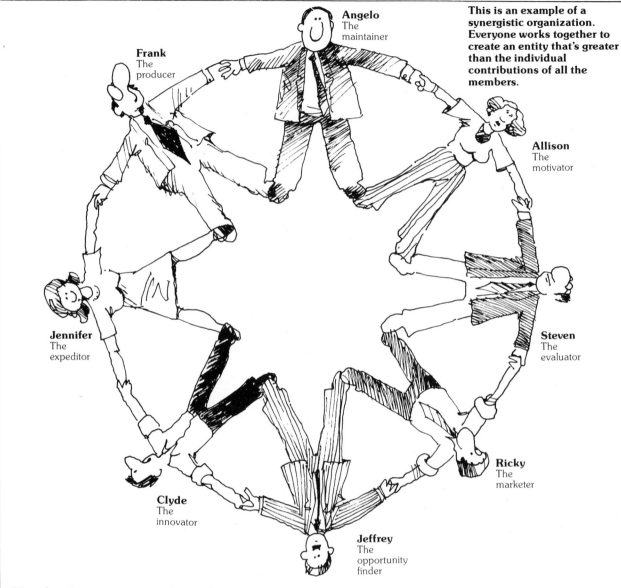

Frank
The producer

Angelo
The maintainer

This is an example of a synergistic organization. Everyone works together to create an entity that's greater than the individual contributions of all the members.

Allison
The motivator

Jennifer
The expeditor

Steven
The evaluator

Clyde
The innovator

Ricky
The marketer

Jeffrey
The opportunity finder

Here's what synergy comes down to:

- A synthesis between individualism and cooperation

- Mutual cooperation for the optimal benefit of all concerned

- A situation where the whole is more than the sum of the parts

- The process of combining the needs of the individual with the needs of the organization—and satisfying those needs better through combined effort than through separate actions

- A social structure that's worth more to belong to than to be separate from

- A relationship that rewards all involved

- A situation where both individual and organization benefit, but neither at the expense of the other

Note: There's a limit to the size of a synergistic organization. The limit is determined by the number of people the manager can effectively relate to personally. As the organization gets more and more people the manager doesn't know, the less and less effective it will be.

Index

5510